WALLS OR BRIDGES

WALLS OR BRIDGES

HOW TO BUILD RELATIONSHIPS THAT GLORIFY GOD

JON JOHNSTON
Foreword by Ted Engstrom

BAKER BOOK HOUSE
Grand Rapids, Michigan 49516

Printed in the United States of America

Scripture references marked NASB are from the New American Standard Bible,
© 1960, 1962, 1968, 1971, 1973, 1975, 1977 by the Lockman Foundation; those
marked NIV are from the New International Version © 1978 by New York
International Bible Society; those marked KJV are from the King James Version;
those marked PHILLIPS are used with permission of the Macmillan Publishing
Company; those marked JB are from the Jerusalem Bible © 1966 by Darton,
Longman & Todd, Ltd. and Doubleday and Company, Inc.; those marked NEB
are from The New English Bible, © 1961, 1970 by The Delegates of Oxford
University Press and The Syndics of the Cambridge University Press.
Those marked RSV are from the Revised Standard Version © 1972 by Thomas
Nelson, Inc.

Library of Congress Cataloging-in-Publication Data

Johnston, Jon.
    Walls or bridges

    Includes indexes.
    1. Interpersonal relations—Religious aspects—Christianity.   I. Title.

BV4509.5.J646   1988   248.4   88–10509

ISBN: 0-8010-5224-6
      0-8010-5223-8 (pbk.)

To

Frank

J. Kenneth

James "Gene"

M.A. "Bud"

Norma

They built bridges
to my life
and
we crossed them
together.

Prayer of Unity

Our Father, we thank you for the privilege of being
together at this time and in this place.

As your people, we pray that your love will unite
us into a fellowship of discovery.

Cleanse us of everything that would sap our
strength for togetherness.

Unravel the knots in our spirits.
Cleanse the error of our minds.
Free us from the bondage of our negative
imaginations.

Break down the barriers that sometimes keep us
apart and cause us to drift along without a
dream.

As we go from here,
Explode in us new possibilities for service.
Kindle within us the fires of your compassion so
that we may not wait too long to learn to love.

May we be a people with loving purposes
Reaching out . . .
Breaking walls . . .
Building bridges . . .

Let us be your alleluia in a joyless, fragmented
world.

In the name of our Lord we pray
Amen.

Earl Lee

Contents

Foreword

Am I—are you—building walls or bridges? Jon Johnston poses this crucial question, the answer to which can result in life-changing, redemptive improvements in our lives.

Footbridges, drawbridges, the Golden Gate bridge, covered bridges, and causeways all bring great lessons concerning our relationships.

The Bible, God's manual for our daily living, has much to say about relationships. God himself established these: heavenly Father—obedient Son; husband-wife; parent-child; friend—neighbor.

We are reminded that Jesus built bridges so durable that they have lasted for two millennia, and so diverse that they connect all human beings with his Father.

Our Lord, the architect of rewarding, Christian relationships, guides us in the important process of tearing down walls and building bridges.

In our day of microwave cooking, fast-food restaurants, condensed seminars and fifteen-second commercials, we need to realize that meaningful relationships require time and energy. Author Johnston wisely brings this to our attention.

This book comes alive with the graphic imagery of walls and bridges. There's nothing stodgy in the author's scriptural references and applications.

The biblical principles—helpfully and interestingly applied in the book—will make better people of us. Our lives will become more fulfilled, enjoyable, and productive.

Jon Johnston, as in the previous books he has written, exhibits a marvelous sense of humor. I was amazed to come across terms like "flakes," "nerds," "bozos," and "klutzes." You will chuckle as did I. They are specimens of life's "irregular" people whom we all encounter. And bridges can be built to them as well. The author helps us to see this, and guides us in the process.

When you finish this book, I predict you will be determined to be a bridge builder. Expect to become a better, stronger person as a result.

Interestingly, this is the first book I have ever read in which helpful footnotes attracted my attention and demanded my reading them!

One word describes this book for me: captivating. See if you don't agree.

Ted W. Engstrom
President Emeritus
World Vision, International

Introduction

It began as a typical, crisp fall day in Malibu. Nothing special occurred—that is, until I attended our morning chapel.

The speaker, a former missionary to India and current minister to a church of several thousands, mesmerized students and faculty alike with his words.

He disclosed that his son was among the Americans being held captive in Iran. To most of us, he had every right to be angry and bitter. Many of us were, and we didn't even have a member of our family imprisoned. But not Earl Lee.

His message was one of forgiveness and understanding. Get this: He even spoke of his love for the Ayatollah Khomeini. We thought, tolerance maybe. But love? Isn't that carrying our Lord's Sermon on the Mount a little too far? Earl Lee showed us that it wasn't.

The world news services had caught wind of his startling declarations in recent weeks. News reporters now jammed into his worship services in order to film his sincere prayers for this nation's hated enemies.

On this particular morning, our speaker began to unroll his large American flag. The same one he raised daily above his house and would until the hostages were released. It symbolized his lofty faith.

It was then that he cast his deep sentiments in a simple, but powerful, theme: Walls or Bridges. And what he said made a lot of sense.

In short, he declared that in all we do and say, we are either building walls or building bridges between ourselves and others. We're putting up roadblocks or we're establishing linkage.

This process is often unconscious, misunderstood, or minimized in our thinking. Nevertheless, it occurs with regularity and great significance.

Well, I left chapel that day with a kindled spirit. The theme remained in my mind as I thought about its implications for my life.

Providentially, it wasn't long before I ran across Gloria Evans' book entitled, *The Wall: A Parable*. And her thoughts were along the same line. Walls protect, but they also imprison. Freedom can only occur when walls are destroyed.

At this point several questions entered my mind. Am I building more walls than bridges? When I construct bridges, are they of the right kind? And do I use them for the right purposes?

This fact is certain: The quality of our relationships is an important barometer of our spiritual well-being. When we turn off others, by intent or neglect, three reputations suffer: our own, that of the body of believers, and most important, the reputation of Jesus Christ.

Those of us who claim to be twice-born must understand the dynamics of godly relationships. Then, with God's guidance and power, we must demolish unsightly walls in order to construct bridges to other people, regardless of our temperament or talent.

Walls or Bridges attempts to encourage us in this necessary task. It is primarily addressed to those of us who love Jesus and who earnestly desire to live for him.

The book's three sections focus on the key components of bridge building.

Section one, "Healthy Relationships," invites us to construct reliable structures. Ones that will stand the tests of change and adversity.

Section two, "Holistic Relationships," focuses on the issue of destination. To where should our bridges reach?

Finally, section three, "Holy Relationships," pertains to the use of our bridges. After building strong, well-constructed bridges and making certain they link us to the right banks, we must begin transporting cargo. Otherwise, our bridges are merely lavish monuments.

What, specifically, must our bridges transport? The biblical answer is emphatic: the Fruit of the Spirit.

May our hearts prayerfully examine these dimensions, and may the Holy Spirit probe us until we respond in obedience.

Part 1

Bridges/Design
Healthy Relationships

The rich man thinks of his wealth as an impregnable defense, a high wall of safety. What a dreamer!
–Proverbs 18:11 LB

People are lonely because they build walls instead of bridges.—Joseph Fort Newton

A flea and an elephant walked side-by-side over a bridge. Said the flea to the elephant after they had crossed, "we sure did shake that thing, didn't we!"

1

Our Chief Demolition Expert and Architect

After our Southern California wedding, Cherry and I jumped into our heaterless Rambler and headed for Kansas City, where I planned to enter seminary.

Enroute, we ran into a blinding rainstorm, necessitating an extra night on the road. As a result, our meager cash supply was evaporated. But we were much too naive to worry.

Finally, we reached our destination, exhausted and broke. Not knowing a soul in town, we resorted to telephoning the seminary president to explain our plight. He rushed over to convey his condolences and to loan us ten dollars.

Jobs were eventually located. I say "jobs," because each was so low paying that we had to work at several. In addition to being a nighttime bill collector in an ethnic section of the city, I played the organ for a local funeral home. Praying for funerals to occur, somehow never did seem right!

We moved into a one-room studio apartment, located above an old garage next to Tower Park. It was actually two rooms, if you counted the wardrobe closet which became my study when the clothes were pushed back.

Unfortunately, our landlord refused to fumigate. This delighted the enormous cockroaches. I recall hearing them walk across the linoleum floor at night. A high percentage of our grocery bill went for insecticide.

The landlady was an early riser. Her morning ritual began about 5 A.M., when she began cranking the starter on her antique Oldsmobile. Finally, the gas-guzzling engine would start, and she would race it for another ten minutes. Great quantities of carbon monoxide fumes would seep through the porous floor of our apartment. One good thing: The fumes did help us with the roach problem!

After a few weeks, our material needs began to be satisfied. We became quite content with our substandard living.

But then it hit us. We became painfully aware of our unmet social needs. We discovered that we were very lonely in this strange city, and it was then that we began groping for friendship. Since others refrained from inviting us to their homes, we decided to do the inviting. The results were as surprising as they were enlightening. Allow me to share three instances.

The first seminarian couple was invited to dinner. Prior to their coming, they expressed a definite preference for coffee. Not being coffee drinkers ourselves, we were forced to experiment. Cherry brewed and tasted coffee the entire day before our guests arrived. They came. One sip of my wife's coffee was enough. It was definitely *not* to their liking. Not only that. My well-intentioned wife was so saturated with caffeine that she lay awake staring at the ceiling the entire night!

Soon thereafter, we focused our attention on another couple, who were overheard complaining about their sad financial plight. We were far from affluent, but felt a strong compulsion to extend a helping hand. After all, these people were described as destitute.

They arrived, and we all enjoyed a scrumptious meal. Then, a couple of weeks later, we were overjoyed to receive an invitation to their home for dessert. Upon arrival, we discovered that they owned a horse-sized dog. All varieties of dog food known to man were piled high on their kitchen table. It wasn't long before a dim light turned on in our naive brains. We realized that destitution is a very relative term.

But it was our third attempt to reach out that took the cake! This couple had been having serious marital problems. It was the Christmas season, and Cherry once again prepared a delicious meal. She even displayed some homemade, festive decorations for the occasion.

The couple entered our humble abode accompanied by their pug-nosed little girl. The catastrophe began. For starters, the youngster began making deep furrows in the maple coffee table with a brass candleholder. After receiving a mild rebuke from her father, the mother and child began repeating these words in unison: "Daddy is a dumb-dumb."

Bored with that, the small aggressor began unwrapping the Christmas presents under the tree. The suspense of wondering what we were getting that year quickly subsided! Both parents laughed convulsively as the gift contents were revealed.

After completing this demolition project, the miniature delinquent disappeared into our bathroom. While we visited, it became apparent to me that she had been in there much too long, even though it was actually no more than five minutes. Her mother decided to check on her well-being. What she saw made her go into hysterical laughter.

Unable to find any small boats or ducks to play with, the sweet young thing had taken my toothbrush and was floating it in the toilet! This time I couldn't help myself. I began to laugh—while grinding my teeth.

More Lesson Than Loss

Cherry and I had attempted to reach out for meaningful relationships. To build a few bridges.

The results were disastrous. In the first instance, we were embarrassed. In the second, we met deception. As for the last instance, we beheld a complete lack of respect for our property. Tell me. Would you have used that toothbrush again?

Our first reaction was to bow out of the bridge-building enterprise. Furthermore, we considered building some walls of our own, or at least some fences. It was Robert Frost who declared, "Good fences make good neighbors."

Good *neighbors*, maybe, but how about good *Christians*? After coming to our senses, we realized that even fence building can yield great spiritual damage. For in reality, fences are thin walls. And all walls have these functions. To break contact. To block communication. To keep what is inside inside. And what is outside outside.

Our physical world is already overdosed on walls! Probably more time, energy, and resources have gone into wall building than any other activity. There are

> Long walls like the ancient one in China, which appeared as "earth's giant necklace" to lunar astronauts.[1]

1. This defensive barrier, erected by China's first Emperor, Qin Shi Huang, extends 3,700 miles from the Gulf of Bohai to the Gansu Province. Actual construction began during the Warring States period in the fifth century B.C. to ward off plundering nomads from the north. After Qin conquered and became the first emperor of a unified China (221 B.C.), he told general Meng Tian to link up these walls and to extend them. Three hundred

Short walls—the kind that border my backyard where flowering vines climb at will, along with tomcats.

Thick walls like those that surrounded Nebuchadnezzar's Babylon[2] and Alexander's Athens.[3]

Thin walls—the kind we've referred to as fences, which broadcast an emphatic "Keep Out!" to neighbors.

Admittedly, some walls are greatly venerated. The Western Wall where Jerusalem's devout pray.[4] And the

---

thousand people did the work. Reinforcement and renovation was carried out during successive dynasties.

Building a wall of this length and magnitude over mountain peaks, precipices and ravines was a stupendous undertaking. Moving stories connected with it reflect the misery it inflicted on the people. Since persons who died while working on it were buried beneath it, the Great Wall has been termed "the largest graveyard in the world." *Sixty Scenic Wonders in China* (Beijing, People's Republic of China: New World Press, 1980), pp. 1–4.

2. King Nebuchadnezzar II erected the three hundred-meter Procession Road (also called Feast Road) in 580 B.C. that led to the spectacular city of Babylon. It was lined on both sides by walls made of colored enamel bricks. Lions (holy animals of the Ishtar religion worshipers, goddesses of love, fertility and war) were etched in the glazed, blue walls. Also, there were dragons and bulls. The main gate to the city was called the Ishtar Gate. The front of the two gate towers has been located, refurbished, and moved to the Pergamum Museum in East Berlin, where it can be seen today (along with thirty meters of the Procession Road). It is a spectacular sight indeed!

3. Like most cities of the ancient world (except for arrogant Sparta), Athens built formidable walls of protection. They extended around their glorious city, and during their Golden Age ruled by Pericles, they extended side-by-side down to the seaport city of Pireas, which was also enclosed by walls. Such walls made Athens seem to would-be enemies almost impregnable.

4. The Western (or Wailing) Wall has been described as a "grim, gray, hyssop-tufted, architectural fragment." It towers about sixty feet above what was once a narrow, ninety-foot-long, stone-paved courtyard.

Jewish tradition maintains that this portion of the wall is the one remnant left of the containing wall of the outermost enclosures of Herod's Temple that has survived war and the elements. Many believe that when God's Shekinah Presence left the Holy of Holies of the Temple (at its destruction), the divine presence went to this section of the Western Wall and hovers over it to this day. As a result, Jews of all types gather there to pray, or send money to have others pray for them. Often prayers are written on notes and stuck in a crevice of the wall.

The Jews were shut out from this, their most sacred place of prayer, for nineteen years from 1948–1967. On June 6, 1967, when the Israeli army was recapturing ancient Jerusalem, their first act was to take the Temple Mount, then to march straight for the Western Wall to kiss its hallowed stones and weep. Today, the Western Wall, especially on Friday afternoons (the evening of the Jewish Sabbath) and on special holy days, is inundated with crowds of worshipers. G. Frederick Owen, *Jerusalem* (Kansas City, MO: Beacon Hill Press, 1972), pp. 106–110.

granite one that names 58,023 Americans who died in
Viet Nam.[5] And then there are walls that only reflect hate
and anger. Like the barbed, grotesque, graffitied Berlin
Wall, which has become a symbol of heartbreak. It seems
only yesterday that Cherry and I stood beside it at Check-
point Charlie and soberly reflected on the unbelievable
trauma it has caused. Divided families. Tragic escape
attempts. Broken dreams.[6]

When it comes to physical walls, a lot of negative
thoughts come to mind. perhaps that's why we have the
expressions "I feel walled-in;" "up against a wall;" "about
to climb a wall."

If this is true concerning physical walls, how much
more is it so regarding the walls that block personal
relationships.

Walls Do a Prison Make

In a classic poem titled "Walls Do Not a Prison Make,"
the author seems to be implying that walls aren't always
incarcerating. Perhaps so. But more often they do imprison.

First, walls can separate us from God. 2 Corinthians
10:3–5 (NASB) tells us how:

> For though we walk in the flesh, we do not war according
> to the flesh, for the weapons of our warfare are not of the
> flesh, but divinely powerful for the destruction of for-

5. The Vietnam Veterans Memorial Wall has been established on the mall in Washington, DC This is a 494-foot monument visited by thousands daily.

6. On August 13, 1971, a wall was built by the East Germans to separate East and West
Berlin. It began with barbed wire, then stone, finally concrete. Today, it is heavily guarded
by fifty thousand soldiers, wolfhounds, and land mines. The form of the wall varies,
sometimes even being the side of a building. Numerous escapes have been attempted, such
as hiding in car trunks, tunneling underneath, riding a balloon over. Prior to the wall's
construction, hundreds of thousands of East Germans crossed over to freedom. The East
German government felt that it could no longer tolerate such a mass exodus; thus, the wall
was constructed to form an imprisoning ring around West Berlin. Rainer Hilderbrandt, *It
Happened At The Wall* (Berlin, 1984), N.P.

tresses. *We are* destroying speculations and every lofty thing raised up against the knowledge of God, and *we are* taking every thought captive to the obedience of Christ.

Paul uses military terms to convey the kind of warfare that takes place in our minds.

In ancient times cities were constructed inside thick, massive walls.[7] Aspiring invaders were deterred by such protective shields. Towers were strategically built into or inside the walls, and from them defenders could pinpoint the locations of advancing troops.[8]

For enemies to take these well-fortified cities, they had to accomplish these three objectives:

1. Walls must be demolished or scaled.[9]

2. Towers must be invaded.

3. Men who planned military strategy must be killed or captured.

If these tasks were completed, victory to the enemy was assured. The battle was over!

The Scripture passage above illustrates this first-century warfare strategy. Author Charles Swindoll explains how it is a symbol of our own struggles.

---

7. Every ancient city had enormous walls surrounding it. Some walls contained chambers inside. There still exist some of the stones in the wall of the Temple enclosure at Jerusalem. They measure thirty feet long, eight feet wide, and three and a half feet high, weighing over eighty tons. *The Zondervan Pictorial Bible Dictionary*, Merrill C. Tenney, ed. (Grand Rapids, MI: Zondervan Corporation, 1963), p. 885.

8. Along the three thousand seven hundred miles of the Great Wall of China, there are massive watchtowers situated every few hundred yards.

Also in Jericho, reputed to be the oldest city in the world, archeologists have unearthed a nine thousand-year-old watchtower. It set back from the ancient wall, because people attached their homes to the latter, making it one side of their abodes. Most probably, it was in such a structure Rahab lived, and because of its proximity to the wall, she was able to help the two Israeli spies escape (Josh. 2).

9. According to our Israeli guide, unless they planned to demolish a city, the Roman soldiers did not pound the walls of a defending army with hammers. Instead, they simply dug away the earth under the wall, causing the entire structure to collapse.

Similarly, our God has no trouble destroying our walls, no matter how formidable they seem to us. He strikes them at the base by changing our hearts and minds.

He says that originally our minds were "enemy-held territories."And, we declare, "Surely I have been a sinner from birth, sinful from the time my mother conceived me" (Ps. 51:5; cf. Rom. 3:23). But then we suddenly became aware of God's love invasion taking place (cf. John 3:16). The enemy within us met his match and was forced to relinquish his control and power.[10]

But we've all found Satan to be an unbelievably determined enemy. He isn't quickly or easily conquered. He retreats fighting. Only with the greatest reluctance does he release his strong hold.

This is evidenced in the stubborn persistence of impure habits, which were deeply embedded in our natures when he controlled us. Paul vividly expresses this reality: "What I want to do I do not do . . . For I have the desire to do what is good, but I cannot carry it out" (Rom. 7:15b, 18b).

10. I feel that the Scriptures support the idea of dealing with our sin in two steps. First, we invite God into our lives through sincere confession. Past sins are acknowledged, then repented of (2 Cor. 7:10, Acts 17:30). We promise to do an about-face—to begin the new life of love (2 Cor. 5:17, Eph. 4:22–24). Then we accept by faith that we are forgiven (Rom. 10:9–10), based on the promise of God's infallible Word (1 John 1:9). The Holy Spirit confirms the reality of this in our hearts (Rom. 8:16–17). Result: We know that we've been born again. We are pardoned rebels.

Second, at a subsequent time we consecrate our forgiven lives to God. We surrender our will to his will. Such consecration is thorough and complete.

It was what Paul wished for the Thessalonians when he declared. "May God himself, the God of peace, sanctify you through and through. May your whole spirit, soul and body be kept blameless at the coming of our Lord Jesus Christ" (1 Thess. 5:23).

Paul's audience had already been born again. He previously spoke of their "work produced by faith," their "labor prompted by love," their "endurance inspired by hope" (1:3). He referred to them as "brothers loved by God" who had been "chosen" (1:4), "imitators of us and of the Lord; in spite of severe suffering" (1:6), and "a model to all the believers in Macedonia and Achaia" (1:7). He declared that he thanks God because they "received the word of God" and "accepted it" fully (2:13). The Thessalonians were forgiven sinners! Nevertheless, the Apostle beckons them to the second work of grace, namely entire sanctification.

In receiving this second gift, our sinful nature is instantaneously cleansed. Our original sin (in contrast to past sins that were forgiven in confession), which is inherited from Adam, is completely removed. We are purged of all uncleanness. More than pardoned rebels, we become intimate, obedient (though yet maturing) children of God—his transformed creation (cf. Rom. 12:1–2).

Our mighty conqueror rescued the apostle from his imprisonment, so that he could triumphantly declare, "Therefore, there is now no condemnation...because through Christ Jesus the law of the Spirit of life set me free from the law of sin and death" (Rom. 8:1–2; cf. Rom. 6:6).

Likewise, Christ desires to liberate all of us from Satan's power. His strategy is clearly outlined in 2 Corinthians, Chapter 10 (NASB).

1. He destroys "fortresses" and "speculations" (v. 4–5). These are walls encircling the mind—habits of thinking ingrained by Satan over the years, destructive, painful mindsets that especially inflict persons who have come to Jesus late in life. (Example: believing that we should punish our persecutors.)

2. He demolishes "every lofty thing raised up against the knowledge of God" (v. 5). These are mental blocks we've erected against spiritual viewpoints, carnal attitudes that typically intensify when we are under pressure and when we see our significant others reacting in sinful ways. (Example: blaming God for our misfortune.)[11]

3. His ultimate goal is to take "every thought captive to the obedience of Christ" (v. 5.). After striking down the old, he proposes to make all new. Romans 12:2 says, "Be transformed by the renewing of your mind." "His plan is to transform old thoughts that

---

11. Roger von Oech has written a book entitled *A Whack on the Side of the Head*. In it he lists ten common statements that hold us back from being what God would have us be. They cast gloom on our faith, and poison the atmosphere with a negative spirit. They are as follows: (1) The right answer. (2) That's not logical. (3) Follow the rules. (4) Be practical. (5) Avoid ambiguity. (6) To err is wrong. (7) Play is frivolous. (8) That's not my area. (9) Don't be foolish. (10) I'm not creative.

Roger von Oech, *A Whack on the Side of the Head* (New York: Warner Books, Incorporated, 1983), p. 9. Quoted in Charles Swindoll, *Living Above the Level of Mediocrity: A Commitment to Excellence* (Waco, TX: Word Books, 1987), p. 25.

defeat us into new thoughts that encourage us."[12]
And he realizes that this means repatterning our
whole way of thinking. (Example: knowing that God
desires the very best for our lives.)[13]

Second, in addition to separating us from God, walls
barricade us from one another.

In her book *The Wall: A Parable*, Gloria Evans testifies
to this fact.

One day I realized that [my] wall was so high that I no
longer saw anyone go by. I no longer heard anyone. Everything was quiet. "Is anyone there?" I yelled. There was no
answer. It was dark inside the wall and the air was foul. I
sat there for a long time. It was quiet and dark and lonely.
Only the whispers of my memories could be heard.[14]

The walls that we build to isolate ourselves from others
refuse to remain stationary. They seem to inch their way
inward, aggressing our life space, invading our consciousness, inflicting discomfort on our daily existence.

It reminds me of the retractable walls used by the
Romans for capital punishment. Criminals were placed in
a room and the mobile walls came inward, one inch each
day. At one point they began touching the skin. Then, a
day or two later, bones were heard cracking along with
muffled screams.

In a similar way, the walls we erect turn on us. The
threat gets closer, inch-by-inch, until we become spiritual
casualties.

Cherry and I decided to resist the temptation to build

---

12. The word Paul uses for being transformed from the world is the Greek term,
metamorphousthai. Our word *metamorphisis* is derived from the same root meaning. It
implies the taking on of a completely new nature. We cease being "worms" and become
beautiful "butterflies."

13. Many of the ideas related to this point, that walls separate us from God, are taken
from the book previously referred to by Charles Swindoll, *Living Above the Level of
Mediocrity: A Commitment to Excellence.*

14. Gloria Jay Evans, *The Wall: A Parable* (Waco, TX: Word Books, 1977), n.p.

walls where our fellow seminarians were concerned. We saw that our only hope was to continue building bridges, even though our first three had collapsed.

How does bridge constructing differ from wall building?

Spanning Gaps and Gulches

Bridges—the kind made of wood and steel—appeared much later in history than walls.[15] And they are not nearly as plentiful.

There are reasons for that. Bridges usually cost more and are more difficult to construct. They require a greater variety of less accessible, more expensive materials.

Also, their upkeep is more necessary and tedious. When a wall collapses (usually only during an earthquake or a military attack), few of us take notice. But when a bridge crumbles, that is a different story.

Approximately 150 bridges in our country give way each year. The results are tragic. Also, it is estimated that one-fifth of our half-million bridges are unsafe. Hearing this fact alarms us much more than learning that 100,000 walls are unsturdy.

In contrast to walls that barricade and block, bridges help to join, connect, reach, link, and bring together.

They also add beauty to our natural environment. We need only to catch a glimpse of San Francisco's Golden Gate as it glistens jewellike in the sun and morning fog.[16]

---

15. The word *bridge* is not found in the English Bible. Nevertheless, the earliest idea of a bridge must have been suggested by a plank or fallen tree across a small stream. But the Israelites generally crossed a stream by a ford (Gen. 32:22, Josh. 2:7, Judg. 3:28) or in some cases by a ferryboat (2 Sam. 19:18, LB).

Although the arch principle was known early, as seen in two stones leaning against each other to bridge a small gap in Myceanaean ruins, it wasn't until the time of the Roman Empire that the magnificent arches, bridges and aqueducts appeared, at which time the bridge may be said to have come into its own. Merril C. Tenney, ed., op.cit. p. 132.

16. The Golden Gate Bridge was opened May 22, 1937. It spans 4,200 feet, connecting San Francisco and Marin Counties. The bridge was designed by Joseph Strauss, with two cables three feet in diameter. Each of these contains 27,572 wires. *Encyclopedia Americana*, Vol. 7, (Grolier, Inc., 1985), p. 532.

But all bridges, in spite of their beauty, size or composition—once again—share the same function, establishing linkage. So that what's over there can come here, and what's over here can go there. So that interchange can occur, whether it be transportation or communication. So that a connection can exist between separate parts.

The same can be said for those bridges that link us as human beings. Social bonding is essential. Even for our physical health. Epidemiologist Lisa Berkan's study of seven thousand persons between the ages of thirty and sixty-nine over a nine-year period reveals that extroverts (bridge builders) are more likely to live longer than introverts (wall builders). Gregarious persons are more resistant to heart and circulatory diseases, cancer and strokes, and less inclined to suicide.

John Donne is right; "No man is an island." So is well-known author Reuben Welch, who declares: "We really do need each other."[17] For fulfillment. For survival. Yet, many of us who realize this fact continue building walls. Walls that separate, seal off, and stifle.

Back to our seminary days. After we committed ourselves to building bridges, some very encouraging things occurred.

Those we reached out to came to learn that our bridges were meant to be permanent. Not like the pontoon kind used to help army troops cross a river. That kind is quickly put down, and then, just as quickly picked up. Our bridges were meant to stay. And when others became assured of this fact, they began to build permanent bridges toward us. And, we met somewhere in the middle.

Once linked up, we joined in mutual efforts to strengthen and reinforce the relationships. They became projects of constant upgrading. By the end of our three years at seminary, some very strong friendships had

---

17. Refer to Reuben Welch, *We Really Do Need Each Other* (Nashville, Impact, N.D.).

formed. And they are still very much intact today, having stood the test of time.

Perhaps it will be helpful to contrast the specifics of wall and bridge building. Here are the essential differences:

Wall Building	Bridge Building
primarily motivates us to *protect ourselves*	primarily motivates us to *help others*
focuses on *hoarding* what we have accumulated	focuses on *sharing* what God has entrusted to us
leads to a self that is *sealed off, ingrown, shriveled*	leads to a self that is *unleashed, outgoing, expanding*
causes us to see others as a *threat* to our security, but worthy of our impressing them.	causes us to see others as *essential* to our well-being and worthy of our accepting them
greatly *diminishes* our usefulness to God	greatly *enhances* our usefulness to God

I heartily believe the above principles in theory. But I also know that they hold true in practice.

At this point something more important must be fully understood. As Christians, our primary interest in bridge building is not based on a desire to maintain our physical or psychological health. Nor to make our lives more pleasant for ourselves or admirable to others. It's not even based on wanting to add a needed dimension to the lives of the needy.

As commendable as those motivations are, they pale in significance when compared to our primary rationale.

We are drawn to this activity, most essentially, because of the example and teaching of our Lord. It is he who destroys unsightly walls and designs beautiful bridges.

It is with him that we begin. He supplies all guidance, as well as the necessary blueprints.

Our Master Link

Satan prides himself on being the master wall builder of our planet. He constructs tall and thick ones that seem insurmountable. Between us and God. Between us and one another. Why? Because he knows that such isolation destroys our inner spirits and deprives those we might help.

By contrast, our heavenly Father constantly builds bridges. The beautiful rainbow that we behold after a rainstorm, with its fusion of colors, is his "bridge of promise" to all mankind. It testifies to his vow that our earth shall never again be destroyed by the kind of flood experienced by Noah. Genesis 9:8–14 (LB) declares:

> Then God told Noah and his sons, "I solemnly promise you and your children and the animals you brought with you—all these birds and cattle and wild animals—that I will never again send another flood to destroy the earth. And I seal this promise with this sign: I have placed this my rainbow in the clouds as a sign of my promise until the end of time, to you and to all the earth. When I send clouds over the earth, the rainbow will be seen in the clouds."

Then, nearly two thousand years ago, God's own son bridged the great gap between the creator and his creation. Jesus,

> Who, being in very nature God, did not consider equality with God something to be grasped, but made himself nothing, taking the very nature [form] of a servant, being made in human likeness. And being found in appearance as a man, he humbled himself and became obedient to death—even death on a cross! (Phil. 2:6–8).

As a result of this, we can now cross his bridge of mercy and grace and enter the very presence of God with boldness (Heb. 4:16). The middle wall that separated us from

God has been destroyed forever.[18] For this reason we sing these joyful words on Easter:

> Once our blessed Christ of beauty
> Was veiled off from human view,
> But thro suffering, death and sorrow
> He has rent the veil in two.[19]

The veil referred to was the thick curtain that separated the Holy of Holies from all people except the high priest, who made an atonement sacrifice there once each year. So in essence, the veil was a cloth wall that isolated God's presence from his people.

When Jesus died on the cross, that curtain was severed from top to bottom. This symbolizes the fact that now all persons everywhere and for all times have direct access to our Father. All because of our Lord.

But, in addition to the bridge he built to connect mankind with God, Jesus constantly built bridges to the persons he encountered. In doing so, he provided us a clear and wise architectural design for our bridge construction projects.

---

18. Ephesians 2:14 speaks of the "middle wall." This is a picture from the Temple complex which consisted of a series of courts, each one a little higher than the one before—with the Temple itself in the innermost court. First there was the Court of the Gentiles, then the Court of Women, then the Court of the Israelites, then the Court of the Priests, and then the Holy Place. Only into the first of them could a Gentile come. Between it and the Court of the Women there was a wall, or rather a kind of screen of marble. Inscribed into it were tablets that announced that if a Gentile came any farther, he was subject to instant death. In 1871 one of these prohibiting tablets was discovered, and the inscription reads, "Let no one of any other nation come within the fence and barrier around the Holy Place. Whosoever will be taken doing so will himself be responsible for the fact that his death will ensue."

Paul was very familiar with this barrier, for his arrest at Jerusalem—which led to his final imprisonment and death—was due to the fact that he was wrongly accused of bringing Trophimus, an Ephesian Gentile, into the Temple beyond the barrier (Acts 21:28–29).

The intervening wall, with its unpassable barrier, shut the Gentile out from the presence of God. It was that wall that was destroyed when Jesus died for all persons everywhere. William Barclay, The Daily Study Bible: The Letters to the Galatians and Ephesians (Philadelphia: The Westminster Press, 1958), pp. 130–131.

19. Taken from the hymn entitled "The Unveiled Christ." Words and score by N. B. Herrell. (Kansas City, MO: Lillenas Publishing Company, 1972), p. 97.

Let's eavesdrop on an encounter he had with a certain woman from Samaria. It is recorded in the fourth chapter of John's Gospel.

More Than a Wishing Well

Accompanied by his disciples, Jesus journeyed toward his home in Galilee. He stopped at Jacob's well to recoup and get a drink. His disciples left him in order to find some food.

Along came a Samaritan woman to draw water from the one hundred-foot deep well. She was so much of a moral outcast that probably she was prohibited from using the town of Sychar's supply.

In the dialogue that transpired, Jesus attempted to bridge, and she countered by erecting walls.

Jesus began by asking for assistance. "Will you give me a drink?" To ask a direct favor is an excellent means to begin a relationship. She turned in astonishment and informed him that it was inappropriate for a Jew to ask such a favor from a Samaritan. Wall number one firmly in place!

She spoke the truth. No love was lost between the Jews and their neighbors. They remembered how in 720 B.C. the Assyrians had invaded, captured, and subjugated Samaria. Afterwards, they transported most of the population to Media (2 Kings 17:6). In turn, foreigners from Babylon, Cuthah, Ava, Hamath, and Sepharvaim (2 Kings 17:24) were transported into the conquered province. The few Jews who still lived there began to intermarry with the foreign people, which the Jews in Judea saw as unforgivable.[20]

The superiority complex of the Jews over the Samaritans had remained firmly intact until that day. Jesus had overstepped his bounds.

20. In a strict Jewish household even to this day, a marriage between a Jewish son or daughter and a Gentile necessitates the conducting of a funeral service for the "lost" child. Such a person is dead in their minds.

Undaunted, our Lord began constructing another bridge. He spoke of his ability to offer her "living water." She took his statement literally, and threw up another barrier. From a well that collects rainwater? Such a claim was foolish! Who was this man, anyhow? He was purporting himself to be wiser and more powerful than Jacob, whom Samaritans claimed to be their "father."

Jesus kindly overlooked the insinuation.

Up went another wall. She said, in effect, "How can you even talk about drawing any (much less running) water, when you don't even have a bucket?" No doubt, like all travelers, Jesus possessed a leather container to retrieve well water. But his disciples had possibly taken it with them into town.

As before, our Lord calmly went around that barrier in order to proclaim spiritual truth. He spoke of offering her water that would quench her thirst forever! The thirst of her eternal soul!

By this time, she may have had a good idea of what he meant. Nevertheless, she put up another barrier of literalism. Her response was flippant, implying that such a gift would certainly save her a lot of future trips to the well.

How many walls would this woman construct? Could they be penetrated? Could Jesus ever build a bridge that would reach her heart?

By this time he had her curiosity. But now it was time to reveal his lordship. Suddenly he brought her to her senses. The time for verbal byplay was over.

"Go, call your husband and come back," he said. She stiffened, grew serious, and looked shocked. Why? Because now she was forced to see herself. And what she saw was not beautiful.

The maze of walls she had constructed began to crumble. She was forced to cease being trite and defensive. It started with an honest admission. "I have no husband," she told him.

Seeing a crack in her resistance, our Lord was quick to disclose his knowledge of her depravity. He said, "You are right when you say you have no husband. The fact is, you have had five husbands and the man you now have is not your husband."

He affirmed that she had spoken the truth, but not the whole truth. And she now fully realized that this man was a prophet.

But, wouldn't you know it, she just had to put up one more wall. The wall of diversion. In essence, she said, "Let's forget me for a moment. There's this question I've been wondering about. Where is the appropriate place to worship? here in Samaria on Mount Gerizim, or in Jerusalem's Temple on Mount Zion?"

Since she cared enough to ask, Jesus offered a quick but thorough reply. In building bridges, we must table our own agendas at times to respond to the concerns of the other individuals. This is a price that must be paid, and Jesus paid it.

Feeling some guilt, the woman was probably pondering where she should go to give an offering for her sin. In her mind, the only cure for sin was sacrifice. And where it took place was crucial.

The Savior offered another answer she was unprepared for. It mattered not where she went. A special location was not required. Anywhere would do. Then he added that this is not to say that the Jewish nation has no unique place in God's plan for salvation of mankind. Worship need not take place only in Jewish territory, but its special significance as his chosen nation is undeniable.

Jesus knew that the Samaritans were off track. They ignored all but the first five books of the Old Testament. Also, they adjusted Scripture and history to glorify their sacred mountain, Gerizim, claiming that it was the site of Abraham's intended sacrifice of Isaac. Being as inoffensive as he possibly could, our Lord exposed these errors.

Well, by this time, the Samaritan woman was bewildered and overwhelmed by her new vista of truth. It all seemed so amazing. So deep. So far beyond her mental grasp.

Her reaction was to construct a final wall—that of delay. In so many words she declared, "Thanks for the interesting discussion, but it's all too much for my shallow mind. I guess I'll have to postpone my conclusions until the Messiah gets here. Then I can ask him what it all means!"

At last she had focused her attention on the need for the Messiah to disclose truth. Here was our Lord's opportunity to reveal his full identity, to reveal that he was more than a nice and clever man who condescended to converse with passersby and greater than one of the many prophets. He was the authentic Messiah, who cared enough about her to patiently reveal the plan of eternal life.

He bridged. She crossed over. For this to occur, he had to transcend all the barriers. She was a Samaritan. She was living in sin. Reasons enough for him to completely ignore her that day!

But our Lord climbed over, went around, or penetrated each of these barricades. And he replaced each one with a bridge. Final score: Jesus 1, Satan 0.

The Samaritan woman had witnessed a masterful job of bridge building. It was only natural for her to begin constructing some of her own. She ran back to town and beckoned people to meet him, suggesting that he could be the Christ. They came, they believed, and they invited him to remain with them to tell others. He stayed for two eventful days.

Upon Jesus' departure, the people of Sychar delivered their final verdict to the Samaritan woman: "We no longer believe just because of what you said; now we have heard for ourselves, and we know that this man really is the Savior of the world."

Not content to go on hearsay, or to base their belief on her testimony, they ventured to cross the bridge themselves.

And to think, it all began with a simple request for a drink of water!

The Samaritan drew water that day. Today, we can draw lessons from the events that transpired. Lessons from the master bridge builder.

Focusing on his example is the first crucial step in learning the essentials of skillful bridge building. He wisely admonishes, "Take my yoke upon you and learn from me" (Matt. 11:29).

But in addition to his unparalleled example as our chief architect he provides us with a set of reliable and ingenious blueprints for our bridge construction. It's time for us to "check out the specs."

With your help I can advance against a troop; with my God I can scale a wall.—2 Samuel 22:30

Lay on me an anvil, O God. Beat me and hammer me into a crowbar. Let me pry loose old walls.—Carl Sandburg "Prayer of Steel"

[We all have] those moments when the lights are out, . . . the valleys deep, and the walls are high, thick, and cold.
                    —Charles Swindoll in *Growing Deep in the Christian Life*

2

Our Precise Blueprint

As a youth I excelled in all kinds of destruction, but displayed a pitifully small aptitude for worthwhile construction. Though leaving a trail of broken everything in my wake, I couldn't seem to make anything that looked good or worked.

The tree houses, club houses, and dog houses ignominiously collapsed. And the bicycle-built-for-two, engineered with great deliberation and care, ended up a bicycle-built-for-nobody!

Then, one Christmas my parents presented me with an Erector Set. They assumed that even a klutz like their son could follow the simple directions. Besides that, all the construction materials were right there in the box. And they were made of steel.

What occurred? You guessed it. Even an Erector Set couldn't make me look good. My engineering feats underwhelmed everybody. The miniature Eiffel Tower I made was a carbon copy of the Leaning Tower of Pisa. And the Golden Gate Bridge looked like a catastrophe!

With such traumatic memories anchored in my psyche, you can imagine why I pricked up my ears when a colleague began bragging about his son's ingenious construction project.

I learned that the lad and his fifth-grade classmates were challenged to build bridges. And they were restricted to using only toothpicks and glue.

The students were divided into groups, each containing no more than a half dozen. Then each child was assigned to a specific position such as being a designer, architect, construction superintendent, or budget manager.

According to the resourceful teacher, the pivotal position in each group was the architect. The plans had to be precise, clear, and complete.

The children realized this fact in the course of their construction. Some tried to change the blueprints after noticing mistakes. To stop these shenanigans, their teacher covered all architectural drawings with wax paper.

Well, finally all the bridges were finished. And the day of judging had arrived. All structures were required to undergo a weight test. Results? Amazingly, most of the toothpick bridges survived fifteen pounds. The sturdiest one supported twenty-three!

Unfortunately, other structures did not fare so well. One responded to the added weight by popping upward. When the weight was removed, it collapsed. Another buckled rapidly, as a chain reaction of weak links led to a small explosion. Wooden fragments flew everywhere.

While musing over this clever learning experience, I couldn't help thinking about the bridge building we are involved in as Christians. The parallel is remarkable.

His Plan Is Our Purpose

When we fail to build healthy, Christ-centered relationships, it is because of either or both of these reasons:

1. We are *following* the blueprints of the wrong architect, Satan; or

2. We are *failing* to abide by the specifications of the right one, Jesus.

In both cases, the collapse of our relationships is assured. Sooner or later the weight test will reveal the weakness of our structure.

Chapter 1 focused on our wall demolition expert and bridge architect. In this chapter we shall examine the reliable set of blueprints that he offers us. That is essential if our bridges are to be structurally sound.

Where are these blueprints located? In his holy Word. Therein are contained sound, timeless truths that—when obeyed—assure us of authentically Christian relationships. The kind that draw us into close communion with others and into intimate oneness with him.

How can we know for certain that the blueprints contained in God's Word are completely reliable? Because his Word is inspired. This means that its authority is not grounded in the response of the readers, nor in the subjective experience of the writers. Rather, the Bible is absolutely reliable because it comes directly from God.

Paul underscores this point when he announces, "All Scripture is God-breathed [given by inspiration of God, KJV] and is useful for teaching, rebuking, correcting and training in righteousness, so that the man of God may be thoroughly equipped for every good work" (2 Tim. 3:16).[1]

The Bible shapes us up so that we can effectively relate to those around us—for God's good purposes.

---

1. *Eerdman's Handbook to the Bible*, David and Pat Alexander, eds. (Grand Rapids, Mi: William B. Eerdmans Publishing Company), chapter entitled "The Bible Is Different," by David Cousins, pp. 32–36.

And because his Word is truly inspired, its impact on the reader is dynamic. Its words penetrate the deepest recesses of our minds and emotions as it bridges us with other persons in other ages.

Nehemiah, Chapter 8 records that Ezra the scribe read from the law of Moses to the returned exiles in Jerusalem. The people, we are told, "understood the reading." But, in addition, they were "weeping when they heard the words of the law" and made "great rejoicing." Furthermore, they returned the next day to build shelters for the Feast of Tabernacles in obedience to the law's commands. The act of hearing and understanding the Scriptures had aroused their emotions and propelled them to action.

Centuries later, biblical scholar and writer J. B. Phillips describes a similar experience he had while translating the New Testament. "Although I did my utmost to preserve an emotional detachment, I found again and again that the material under my hands was strangely alive; it spoke to my condition in the most uncanny way."

No wonder the Bible's author used vivid metaphors to describe the impact that God's Word had made on their lives. To them it was:

a hammer to break	a fire to warm
water to cleanse	milk to nourish
meat to invigorate	light to guide
a sword for the fight	a mirror to reveal
at work in believers	able to build you up
living	active
piercing	discerning[2]

The conclusion is obvious. When we approach these blueprints, we can expect to be transformed dynamically!

In addition to capturing our aesthetic interests and supplying us with historical and theological information,

---

2. *Ibid.*, chapter entitled "The Bible and Christian Living," by David Field, pp. 48–49.

The scriptural references are as follows: Nehemiah 8, Jeremiah 23:29, 1 Peter 2:2, Hebrews 5:13–14, Psalm 119:105, Ephesians 6:17, James 1:23–25, 1 Thessalonians 2:13, Acts 20:32, Hebrews 4:12.

the Bible has a dramatic impact on our lives. And it links us with people through the centuries who have followed its hallowed pages to align themselves with the Savior's will.

Prep Time

But before we can build bridges, God's plans call for our taking care of those walls. The ones that block us from Jesus and from one another.

Some we need to demolish completely, just as the Roman armies of Titus did to Jerusalem's walls in A.D. 70. I can picture the grotesque-looking battering ram relentlessly doing its destruction.

Walls of sin require such thorough annihilation. Walls bearing the identity of anger, greed, envy, jealousy, prejudice, strife, and the like must be destroyed. Romans 6:6 (KJV) speaks emphatically of this necessity; "Knowing this, that our old man [self] is crucified with *him* [Jesus], that the body of sin might be destroyed."

But there are other walls we encounter that are not inanimate, walls involving the entrenched wills of stubbornly disobedient persons. For certain, we are not advised to infract their personhoods or transgress their freedom. As someone put it, they were made before we became maker.

Rather, such walls must be transcended. Instead of a battering ram, the ancient siege engine comes to mind.

When armies found a wall too thick to penetrate, they would push a tall, wheeled structure against its surface. Then after climbing to the top, they would extend a bridgelike walkway over the top of the wall, enabling their warriors to cross into enemy territory.

There are times when we Christians must climb over walls that people have constructed. Walls that are intended to shut us out. We must rise above such barriers, just as our Lord did in the story of his conversation with the Samaritan woman at Jacob's well.

But the point remains. Whether it's through or over, we must conquer those walls!

Then, after effectively responding to the wall issue, we are ready to build bridges. And according to the "specs" in God's Word.

So turn up the lamp a bit. Move a little closer and lean down. It's time to take a penetrating look at what is penned in blue ink.

Approach this task with hope and vision, for here before us are God's plans for guiding us into the kinds of relationships that we need.

Descendants of Aaron; That's Us!

In Old Testament times, all priests were descendants of Aaron, the brother of Moses who performed priestly duties during the period of the Exodus. Also, in each generation the legal head of the house of Aaron came to be called the high priest.

Then Jesus came, and everything changed. Especially the idea of priesthood.

The Lord himself became the one high priest. Hebrews explains this so well: "We have a great high priest . . . Jesus the Son of God . . ." (4:14). Continuing, the writer declares:

> Such a high priest meets our need—one who is holy, blameless, pure, set apart from sinners, exalted above the heavens. Unlike the other high priests, he does not need to offer sacrifices day after day, first for his own sins, and then for the sins of the people. He sacrificed for their sins once for all when he offered himself. For the law appoints as high priests men who are weak; but the oath, which came after the law, appointed the Son, who has been made perfect forever (7:26–28).

Because of this reality, all of us who are his servants can legitimately claim to be authentic priests. As Martin

Luther said in the statement that became the rallying cry for the Reformation, there is a "priesthood of *all* believers."

This is true because our blueprint says so. Revelation says, "To him who loves us and has freed us from our sins by his blood, and has made us to be . . . priests to serve his God and Father" (1:5b–6). Again: "You [Jesus] have made them [Christians] to be . . . priests to serve our God, and they will reign on the earth" (5:10; cf. 20:6).

But it is Peter who lays this truth before us in a very picturesque fashion:

> As you come to him [Jesus], the living Stone—rejected by men but chosen by God and precious to him—you also, like living stones, are being built into a spiritual house to be a holy priesthood, offering spiritual sacrifices acceptable to God through Jesus Christ (1 Peter 2:4–5).

Question: What does the fact of our priesthood have to do with our relationships? Plenty. The Latin word for priest is *pontifex* which means—you guessed it—"bridge builder."

The fact that we're all priests, obedient to our one high priest, means that our mission is to form linkages with others. But even more important, to link others with him. Just as our great high priest bridged us with his Father through his death.

So congratulations to all of us, the spiritual descendants of Aaron. We are charged with the awesome responsibility and offered the great privilege of being card-carrying members of his bridge-building union. Moreover, our Lord has fully paid—once and for all—our union dues!

To realize these truths is to give ourselves the green light. To admonish ourselves to discover just *how* our blueprint instructs us to relate as priests. Let's explore with open minds and hearts.

After prayerfully scrutinizing God's Word, it becomes apparent that two main planks must support the bridges that we build as Christians. Two undergirding principles are completely reliable, consistent, practical, achievable, all because of Jesus. What are they?

1. Compassion: An Eraser on a Pencil?

Former Vice President Hubert Humphrey had a unique way of expressing himself. Speaking to a group of Christian men while holding a long pencil, he said, "Gentlemen, just as the eraser (on this pencil) is only a very small part...and is used only when you make a mistake, so compassion is only called upon when things get out of hand." He concluded by saying, "The main part of life is competition; only the eraser is compassion.... In politics, compassion is just part of the competition."[3]

But that was Hubert Humphrey talking. Our blueprint considers compassion to be much more than an eraser. It's that too, all right, but much more.

Compassion is a quality of spirit highly valued by our Lord. The Gospel writer tells us, "When he saw the crowds, he had compassion on them, because they were harassed and helpless, like sheep without a shepherd" (Matt. 9:36). Then, in Luke 6:36 Jesus says to his disciples, "Be merciful [compassionate] just as your Father is merciful."

The word *compassion* is derived from the Latin words *pati* and *cum*, which together mean "to suffer with." To be compassionate means to enter the arena of pain, to share in brokenness and anguish, to cry out with those in misery.

We're quite willing to speak down to and advise those who suffer. After all, they are flat on their faces because of their own faults, we often think.

But the compassion Jesus speaks of and demonstrated so faithfully has nothing to do with this kind of insulting

---

3. Donald P. McNeill, Douglas A. Morrison, Henri J.M. Nouwen, *Compassion: A Reflection on the Christian Life* (Garden City, NY: Image Books, 1966), p. 6.

paternalism. He would, most likely, tell us to spare the needy our platitudes and advice that would only intensify their hurt.

Some of us are willing to reach down to the destitute in order to pull them up to our level. We're so noble.

Again, our Lord expects more than this expression of pity. For such an attitude masks inherent feelings of superiority. He'd likely tell us to forget such "favors," especially the once-a-year-at-Christmas-kind!

His clarion call is for us to get down with the hurting. To climb down into their trenches. To identify with their misery. And then to lovingly offer his help without expecting a return and without demanding improved performance. Compassion has no preconditions.

I have observed a pervasive hesitancy among Christians to assume such a lowly posture. Self-preservation and even self-ascendancy often seem to be their guiding stars.

This was clearly demonstrated among members of a church at one of their recent meetings. Their spacious, multi-facilitied church building was certainly not being taxed to the limit. Those who came seemed to rattle around in the large structure.

At this particular session, a self-supporting ethnic minister made a polite request to start a new congregation in their building. He assured them that he would worship at nonconflicting times, respect the property, and keep in close contact. Furthermore, he would be willing to pay for his keep.

In spite of these facts, one key board member responded, "If we grant this request, I fear that these people will take us over!" The wall of self- preservation went up, compassion went out the window.

Thankfully, this man's knee-jerk reaction wasn't allowed to prevail. Other members brought the discussion back to biblical basics. The request was granted.

We wince at this example, but how many of us have rejected opportunities for compassion? "Sorry, but I'm really too timid to contact absentees." "I just don't have the stomach for watching those guys at the mission eat." "Give to hungry children overseas? Never. God has given me my own hungry mission field."

Daniel McNeill, in his book entitled *Compassion*, states it well: "Jesus' compassion is characterized by a downward pull." That disturbs us, because we focus on the upward climb as we strive for better lives, higher salaries, more prestigious positions.[4]

Compassion means going directly to those people and places where suffering is most acute and building a home there. Just as Jesus did when he left the portals of paradise to "pitch his tent" among us.

> Who, being in very nature God, did not consider equality with God something to be grasped, but made himself nothing, taking the very nature of a servant, being made in human likeness. And being found in appearance as a man, he humbled himself and became obedient to death—even death on a cross! (Phil. 2:6–8).

Verse five of this convicting chapter says it all: "Your attitude should be the same as that of Christ Jesus." It's really not optional. Filled with his presence, we *must* be compassionate!

2. Community: Come on Board!

Quartets used to sing a toe-tapping ditty entitled "On The Jericho Road." The words begin, "On the Jericho Road, there's room for just two. No more or no less, just Jesus and you."

No way! Last month I traveled on that ancient highway

---

4. *Ibid.*, pp. 26–28. On page 26, the author makes this additional comment: "Instead of striving for a higher position, more power, and more influence, Jesus moves, as Karl Barth says, from 'the heights to the depth, from victory to defeat, from riches to poverty, from triumph to suffering, from life to death.'" [Taken from Karl Barth, *Church Dogmatics*, IV/I (Edinburgh: T and T Clark, Sons, 1956), p. 190.]

and saw for myself. The Jericho Road has room for a lot more than Jesus and you—or me. It will hold thousands.

Too many of our hymns emphasize wrongly, I feel, the isolated believer alone with God. Now, I'm sure that this kind of thinking squares with our go-it-alone culture. Admittedly, all of us do feel like we're in a sealed vacuum at times. And the feeling can get very uncomfortable, as intimated in this poem by Jim Long:

> Sometimes I feel isolated,
>   so completely alone,
>   as if I am entombed
> in a Plexiglass shell.
> I can look out.
> Others can look in.
> But we are separated. . .
> Some people tell me
> I should not have lonely feelings.
> I should climb out of my shell. . .
> as if I can instantaneously
> melt the plastic
> or will the shell to shatter.[5]

But with Jesus, and our brothers and sisters in Christ, it must be different. We're inseparably linked into a compassionate community of believers.

Forget any lonely journey on the Jericho Road. In a very real sense, the Christian's journey is more like what occurred on the Golden Gate Bridge some time ago. The occasion was the fiftieth anniversary of the celebrated structure. And did the people ever come to celebrate!

Over eight-hundred-thousand jammed onto the bridge with noisemakers and flags. Some feared that the tremendous weight might be too much for the old, steel monument. One person said that it did actually buckle a bit, but it held as thousands celebrated.

With Jesus as our reliable bridge, we the very large

5. Poem titled "The Lonely Quiet." Found in loose form, publication unknown.

community of disciples can rest our full weight on him
and continually celebrate en masse. The very thought of
this makes me want to write another song: "On the Bridge
of Jesus Christ, There's Room for Millions." And here's
the best part, as still another songwriter has penned,
"Though millions have come, there's still room for one."

The message of the Bible is that the compassionate life
is a life of living together, rather than being individuals
with isolated personality traits or special talents. Paul
exhorted the Philippian church to live compassionately
in this manner:

> There must be no competition among you, no conceit; but
> everybody is to be self-effacing. Always consider the other
> person to be better than yourself, so that nobody thinks of
> his own interests first but everybody thinks of other
> people's interests instead (Phil. 2:3–4, JB).

How often we focus our attention on individual ac-
claim and personal advancement. Even (and maybe especially) in the church!

Case in point. I've heard persons in the clergy wax
eloquently on the subject of servanthood, rightly saying
that we must be willing to "decrease so that he might
increase."

Yet, somehow, few whom I have known have willingly
taken a step down on the political ladder. Moving to a
small church is almost out of the question. And those
who are elected to administrative posts are even less
prone to relax their power grasp. The very thought of
reentering the pastorate makes them cringe, for it seems
like a backward step. They've become used to the perks,
the power, the privileged position, and others' perceptions of them, too. Admit it or not, they are dug in, though
they might articulate otherwise.

Again, the New Testament admonition is to think
community welfare rather than individual advancement.
Ours is a corporate identity. No wonder our blueprint

uses the term *one another* in no less than thirty distinct manners![6]

And that's why the Good Book makes such a big deal of the term *fellowship*. New Christians after the Day of Pentecost devoted themselves to it (Acts 2:42; cf. 1 John 1:3). This word, in Greek *koinonia*, means two things: first, a "sharing together in partnership," and second, a "giving of what we have (and are) to others." *Union* and *communion*. Such activities are the expected outgrowths of true community.[7]

Compassion and Christian community do not exist in isolation. They have a deep and profound effect on one another.

The first is a God-given quality of heart that makes us want to completely identify with others' suffering. It is an individual matter.

New Testament community, on the other hand, refers to a kind of spiritual melting that makes many compassionate individuals into one, so that they might corpo-

6. The phrase "one another" is employed in the New Testament (NASB) in the following manners: exhort (encourage) one another every day (Heb. 3:13); edify (build up) one another (Rom. 14:19); admonish (instruct) one another (Rom. 15:14); through love be servants of one another (Gal. 5:13); bear one another's burdens and so fulfill the law of Christ (Gal. 6:2); teach and counsel (admonish) one another (Col. 3:16); comfort one another (1 Thess. 4:18); stir (stimulate) one another up to love and good works (Heb. 10:24); confess your sins one to another and pray for one another (James 5:16); offer hospitality to one another without complaint (1 Peter 4:9); be devoted to one another in brotherly love—honor one another above yourselves (Rom. 12:10); don't challenge one another or envy one another (Gal. 5:26); do not be conceited and live in harmony with one another (Rom. 12:16, RSV); be patient, bearing with one another in love (Eph. 4:2); speak truth to one another for we are all members of one body (Eph. 4:25, NIV); be kind and compassionate to one another, forgiving each other, just as Christ forgave you (Eph. 4:32); submit to one another out of reverence for Christ (Eph. 5:21, NIV); don't speak against one another (James 4:11); clothe yourselves with humility toward one another (1 Peter 5:5); if we love (*agape*) each other God lives in us and his love is perfected in us (1 John 4:12); we are members one of another (Rom. 12:5); seek to do good for one another (1 Thess. 5:15); do not lie to one another—there cannot be Greek or Jew, circumcised or uncircumcised . . . but Christ is all and in all (Col. 3:9–13); love one another earnestly from the heart (1 Peter 1:22); care for one another (1 Cor. 12:25); speak to one another in psalms and hymns and spiritual songs (Eph. 5:19); love one another, for love is of God (1 John 4:7); bear with each other and forgive whatever grievance you may have against another (Col. 3:13, NIV); a new commandment I give to you, that you love one another, even as I have loved you (John 13:34); by this all men will know that you are my disciples, if you have love for one another (John 13:35).

7. Jerry Bridges, *True Fellowship* (Colorado Springs: Navpress, 1985), p. 16.

rately respond to God's presence and others' needs. In a day when persons will stop at nothing to get ahead, an authentic Christian community is a refreshing oasis.

Speaking to his diversified audience, Paul announces:

> You are all sons of God through faith in Jesus Christ, for all of you who were baptized into Christ have clothed yourselves with Christ. There is neither Jew nor Greek, slave nor free, male nor female, for you are all one in Christ Jesus (Gal. 3:26–28; cf. John 17:11b).

As his priests, we must continually remind ourselves of our bridge-building function. Our highest goal is to become middlemen, helping his community to grow and become ever more tightly bonded.

In addition to constructing bridges, we must often become bridges ourselves. The imagery is captured in a recent incident that occurred in London.

That's Stretching It a Bit!

United Press International reports the unusual story about a bank official who literally stretched his six-foot-three-inch frame across a gap in order to allow twenty persons to reach safety.

Andrew Parker, seeing his family and other desperate, panic-stricken people stranded on the Zee-brugge ferry in the turbulent English Channel, came up with the emergency plan.

He sized up the situation. Between the sinking ship and a small island of metal was a six-foot-wide cascade of water, which "was too big for people to jump across." So, in Parker's words, "I just made a sort of a bridge."

His wife Eleanor was the first to try out the human structure. She said, "I stepped on his back and I was petrified!"

All of the people made it across. Once across, all of them clung to the small island until rescuers could throw a rope. Parker helped everyone climb the rope.

"People were screaming, and my daughter thought she was going to die," Eleanor Parker declared. "She said, 'Mommy, if I did something wrong, I didn't mean to do it.'"

But, in the midst of all the confusion and pandemonium, hero Andrew became himself a vital link to safety.

Our world is filled with gaps caused by sin. People, though attempting to appear calm, have an internal state of disequilibrium. They impulsively try to span their gaps with structures that are certain to collapse: drugs, alcohol, illicit sexual encounters, gambling. The list seems unending.

Only Jesus can truly satisfy their hearts and ensure their eternal safety. But he needs our help. He has anointed us as his priests, or bridges, to rescue the perishing.

Are we willing to become Andrew Parkers for him?

Well, after becoming thoroughly acquainted with our chief architect and gaining a full understanding of his blueprint, we are ready to collect needed materials. Otherwise, our structure will only remain in the planning stage.

So let's bring on the items that are necessary to build solid and trustworthy relationships.

I will tear down the wall you have covered with whitewash and will level it to the ground so that its foundation will be laid bare.—God to Israel, Ezekiel 13:14

Before I build a wall I'd ask to know
What I was walling in or out.
And to whom I was like to give offense.
Something there is that doesn't love a wall,
That wants it down.
*   —Robert Frost, "Mending Wall"*

The youth gets together his materials to build a bridge to the moon . . . the middle-aged man . . . build(s) a woodshed with them.—Henry David Thoreau

3

Our Essential Construction Materials

Suppose we decided to build an expansion bridge over a wide, raging river, one that would support many heavy vehicles simultaneously.

We'd be certain to select just the right materials. Items such as bailing wire, paper, and scotch tape wouldn't even be considered.

There would be no cutting of corners. We would set out to gather only heavy-duty, reliable materials like cement, steel cable, and granite.

By contrast, if our task were to construct a wall, we wouldn't need to be so particular. We could use almost anything that we could get to stand up: plastic, dirt, block, wood, hedge.

Why the difference? The reasons are obvious.

54

Unlike the wall, our bridge must be made to counteract gravitational pull and to support greater weight.

Also, we realize that the bridge is less likely to survive any flaw or weakness. Remember the old adage, "A chain is no stronger than its weakest link?" The same is true for a bridge. Recall last chapter's toothpick bridge that buckled when one part gave way?

But there is one final reason, and it is the most important. When a bridge collapses, the tragedy is usually more pronounced than when a wall collapses.

For these reasons, it is apparent that great care must go into the selection of bridge-building materials.

The same principle holds for the bridge construction we do as Christians. Only the best materials will do. Why? Because our relationships must counter such gravitational forces as hardship and ill health. They must be able to support excess weight. And, without a doubt, their collapse is sure to yield great trauma to our lives.

How much easier it would be if we were building walls. The materials are cheaper and a lot easier to acquire. No farther away than a thoughtless deed! Some wall-building materials come to mind: an "I-wish-I-could-take-it-all-back" comment; a "make-my-day" hate stare; and "I'll-never-do-it-again-I-promise" affair. All are the stuff that barricades between people are made of.

But, to reiterate, our bridges, if they are to be sound and strong, must be built with only the best materials. We can't afford to scrimp with those that are inferior.

Case in point. Husbands often allow such intruders as "work mania" and "golfitis" to shortchange the quality of materials they invest in their marital relationships. The results are not good.

Often they use inferior materials like cards, candy, and flowers, to make up for noncommitment. Their wives are usually well aware of their antics. Some wives become suspicious and resentful of such counterfeit measures— cheap substitutes for the real thing.

I must add this qualification. The above items are very appropriate for husbands and wives to give to one another. But only if they are seen as supplements to, and not substitutes for the essentials. If they are "added-to," not "instead-of."

The point is clear. All relationships, regardless of their nature, require the costly investment of certain critical materials.

To place these essential items in proper perspective, let's focus on the foundation upon which they must lie.

The Bedrock of Commitment

There are many ways to reveal commitment. At Pepperdine University it is often expressed in "gallows humor."

Allow me to illustrate.

A few years ago, a faculty colleague of mine had his life threatened by a mentally disturbed student. When the news leaked out, our entire campus seemed upset. How would this touchy situation be resolved? The tension mounted.

Then, the faculty member's best friend—an administrator—did a very humorous thing. He made a sign and posted it on his bulletin board. In big, bold letters it read:

> I DO NOT KNOW,
> NOR HAVE I EVER KNOWN
> BOBBY JOE GILLIAM
> NOR DO I THINK THAT I WOULD EVEN LIKE HIM
> IF I KNEW HIM!

In reality, this was only a joke. But it did serve to defuse the tension and assured that his best friend was committed to his well-being.

Humor aside, the *Random House Dictionary* defines commitment as "pledging oneself to" a thing, idea, or person.[1] It carries with it the idea of giving loyalty, resources, and attention in a total, hands-down manner.

Commitment goes much deeper, and is far more intense, than involvement—which implies mere participation with or in. I like the distinction that someone made between these two concepts. "A chicken was involved in my breakfast. She laid the egg. But a pig was truly committed. He furnished the bacon!"

What is commitment really? Think of the bridge again. Commitment is the bedrock far beneath the earth's surface on which is based the giant pilasters that support the superstructure of the bridges. Commitment is solid, strong, immovable.

The image that we receive here is one of *steadfastness*.

Our commitment to Jesus must consist of persevering—stalwart steadfastness—in order for our relationship with him to remain vibrant and intense. Paul says it well. "Stand firm. Let nothing move you. Always give yourselves fully" (1 Cor. 15:58).

When we commit ourselves to him in this way, we are then able to extend Christian commitment to those for whom he died. As a result, we will form the kinds of relationships that please him and make us fulfilled.

But it is important to realize that commitment is a topic that is also increasingly being recognized in our secular society.

Is It Your Heart's Habit?

According to the sociologist-author Robert N. Bellah in his best-selling book titled *Habits of the Heart*, this nation's baby boomers are seriously questioning the value of rugged individualism. A concept that is as American as Coca-Cola and hotdogs (called Dodgerdogs in Los Angeles) at baseball games.

---

1. *The Random House Dictionary*, Jess Stein, editor-in-chief (New York: Ballantine Books, 1980), p. 184.

The sizable and influential segment of our society seems to feel that both the "me generation" (narcissists of the 70s) and the "give-me generation" (materialists of the 80s) have taken individualism to a ridiculous extreme. They see that the results of these decades are rampant self-centeredness and myopia in epidemic proportions.

The only value of relationships is satisfaction of personal needs. If that goal is unmet, relationships are abruptly ended and thrown away with no thought given to their repair.

But refreshingly the author states that the boomers are calling for a return to authentic commitment in their relationships, so that they think "us" instead of "me."

Why do they feel this way? Because there is intrinsic worth in committed bonding. Through it we receive our significance as persons and it almost seems ironic, but we are the ones who receive the greatest payoff for developing committed relationships. Through them we become self-actualized, even though that is not our primary purpose in relating to others.

Implications? According to these young adults, it is time to say no to the pop psychologists who say, "Get in touch with your feelings; focus your attention on number one; go for it all, in order to die with the most toys." That kind of thinking no longer washes with many people.

Baby-boomer marketing consultant, David Wolfe, puts it thus:

> An uncommitted relationship is like living in an emotional amusement park—doing everything for yourself alone quickly burns itself out. I've found that there's no better way to find fulfillment in life than to focus on (i.e., be committed to) . . . (other) persons.[2]

Without commitment our bridge building doesn't stand a chance. With it, regardless of life's weights and

2. Robert N. Bellah et. al., *Habits of the Heart: Individualism and Commitment in American Life* (New York: Harper and Row, Publishers, 1985).

intrusions, survival is assured. And as the late author and educator Bertha Munro says, "We will not merely survive somehow, we'll survive triumphantly!"

Again, we must think of commitment as the supporting principle of our relationships. The other materials are built on this solid foundation.

Thinking of it in another way, each of the remaining materials is an expression of commitment.

Let's turn our attention to these manifestations of Christian commitment.

Start Glancing at Your Watch: Commitment of Time

The other day I wandered into a stationery and party supply store. As I walked down one aisle, I happened upon an entire section of things for a fortieth birthday. There were "It's all over" balloons, black napkins and plates, mourning paraphernalia, and the like. I recalled my recent trip to the local pastry shop, when I saw a fortieth birthday cake decorated with black and moldy-colored green frosting. On top was a tombstone.

It all seemed pretty amusing, that is until I realized that I had recently had *my* fortieth birthday. Then I recalled a statement credited to Winston Churchill: "The age forty may not be the beginning of the end, but it is definitely the end of the beginning."

Where had those years gone? But even more important, had I spent them wisely? All 14,600 days; 350,400 hours; 21,024,000 minutes of them?

Could I really consider myself to have been a faithful steward of my time? More important still, would I buy up my opportunities in a better way during the years that remain?

James 4:14 describes life as "a mist that appears for a little while and then vanishes." It's a simple case of hatch (birth), match (marriage—which is optional) and dispatch (death) in rapid succession.

And so we form cliques. Furthermore, the cliques we form give rise to other cliques—formed by those who resent our cliques. Before long, our churches have so many walled-in cliques that they resemble giant mazes.

Newcomers may vigorously attempt to break into our fellowship, but encountering such barriers is usually enough to generate discouragement and withdrawal.

An elderly couple began attending my own church. They had just moved to California from the hospitable Midwest. Being quite shy themselves, they were very hesitant to make bridge-building overtures. It was their feeling that others should build bridges to them, and they were right, but few if any did.

This continued for over a year. Then, in desperation, this lonely couple began groping for friendship. It was a Sunday evening. The church service had just concluded. The gentleman made a beeline for the targeted couple. After clearing this throat a few times he said, "My wife and I would like to have you join us at a nearby restaurant for a cup of coffee."

The response shot back, "Sorry, but on Sunday evenings we get together only with the same four people— our closest friends!" In other words, not this Sunday night, not next Sunday night, not *any* Sunday night. You're not good enough.

You can imagine the old fellow's reaction. His voice stammered, as he began backing up. After telling his wife, they went home devastated. In relating the story to me, he concluded by saying two words: "We cried."

In spite of our age gap, my wife and I attempted to establish a relationship with them, and we requested other couples to do the same. Fortunately they have, and the couple is becoming accepted as part of the church.

Sure, building new bridges does involve risk. To launch out in faith can, and often does, mean pain. But, as followers of the one who "learned obedience from what he suffered" (Heb. 5:8), we have no other option. To do otherwise is to invite spiritual atrophy and demise.

I heard about a small girl who was suffering in the hospital. In her anguishing moments, someone said to her, "Amy, don't you know that Jesus loves you?" Sobbing, she replied, "But I need someone with skin."

There is no touch like the closeup, personal touch, the intimate encounter where words, actions, and body language can communicate the message "I care." People need people "with skin" to be the virtual incarnation of Christ's love. And many times the most important thing is simply for them to be there and spend time.

Regardless of what we've heard, time does *not* fly. It moves at a steady, consistent pace. Also, there *are* enough hours in the day if we plan studiously and judiciously.

Nevertheless, our time is very limited. As my homespun-philosopher father used to say, "The time that knows us now will soon know us no more." Also, "Our hearts beat like a muffled drum to the grave." But the most memorable statement he used to make was, "We must see all time in the light of eternity."

We must cease pretending that our lives on earth will last forever. This means focusing on people rather than things, on others rather than ourselves.

Bonnie Prudden put it right. "We can't turn back the clock. That is true. But we can wind it up again." Let's do just that, and as we do, I propose that we resolve to commit a lion's share of the future to others!

Begin Relinquishing Your Security: Commitment to Risk

Proverbs 28:1 speaks of the righteous as being "as bold as a lion." We all know that this king of the jungle rarely backs off from a challenge. His bravery is legendary.

As Christians, many of us roar within the protected confines of our churches. But when it comes to risk building *new* bridges for the Lord, we whimper.

Who needs new bridges? The old ones work fine! Old cliques are safe and comfortable. Old friends remain true.

And so we form cliques. Futhermore, the cliques we form give rise to other cliques—formed by those who resent our cliques. Before long, our churches have so many walled-in cliques that they resemble giant mazes.

Newcomers may vigorously attempt to break into our fellowship, but encountering such barriers is usually enough to generate discouragement and withdrawal.

An elderly couple began attending my own church. They had just moved to California from the hospitable Midwest. Being quite shy themselves, they were very hesitant to make bridge-building overtures. It was their feeling that others should build bridges to them, and they were right, but few if any did.

This continued for over a year. Then, in desperation, this lonely couple began groping for friendship. It was a Sunday evening. The church service had just concluded. The gentleman made a beeline for the targeted couple. After clearing this throat a few times he said, "My wife and I would like to have you join us at a nearby restaurant for a cup of coffee."

The response shot back, "Sorry, but on Sunday evenings we get together only with the same four people— our closest friends!" In other words, not this Sunday night, not next Sunday night, not *any* Sunday night. You're not good enough.

You can imagine the old fellow's reaction. His voice stammered, as he began backing up. After telling his wife, they went home devastated. In relating the story to me, he concluded by saying two words: "We cried."

In spite of our age gap, my wife and I attempted to establish a relationship with them, and we requested other couples to do the same. Fortunately they have, and the couple is becoming accepted as part of the church.

Sure, building new bridges does involve risk. To launch out in faith can, and often does, mean pain. But, as followers of the one who "learned obedience from what he suffered" (Heb. 5:8), we have no other option. To do otherwise is to invite spiritual atrophy and demise.

C. S. Lewis in his inimitable style articulates this fact in graphic terms: "Love anything, and your heart will certainly be wrung and possibly be broken. If you want to (keep) it intact, you must give your heart to no one. . . . Wrap it carefully around with hobbies and little luxuries; avoid all entanglements; lock it up safe in the casket . . . of your selfishness. But in that casket—safe, dark, motionless, airless—it will change. It will not be broken; it will become unbreakable, impenetrable, irredeemable. . . . The only place outside heaven where you can be perfectly safe from all the dangers . . . of love is hell."

Rather than waiting for others to approach us and make us feel comfortable, we must take the initiative. Jesus will help us to transcend propensities toward shyness. His Spirit will provide the words to say, and we will improve with practice.

But, once we approach others in love, what should our attitude be?

Make Encouragement Your Goal: Commitment to Affirmation

Robert Schuller said it, and I heartily concur: "Words can either be bombs or baths; bullets or blessings." And whichever they are is of crucial importance to our relationships.

USA TODAY reported the results of a survey of married couples. It was revealed that, while happy and unhappy couples self-disclose equally, the happy couples are characterized by upbeat positive communication patterns.

Those who admitted to being unfulfilled said they spend time alone reflecting on their anxieties, fears, and weaknesses. By contrast, the ones who felt that they had togetherness shared hopes and dreams. They focused on strengths and encouragement.[3]

3. Marilyn Elias, "Happy couples accentuate the positive," *USA TODAY*, p. 10.

Ditto in our churches. "Wet blankets" wreak havoc. It takes five upbeat persons to merely cancel one's gloomy spell. Get enough of these deadbeats, and any bridge-building energy is depleted.

As believers, we are called upon to be bridges over troubled waters. To provide hope and joy. To communicate that we really care. To link those who are discouraged with the master, who says, "Come to me, all you who are weary and burdened, and I will give you rest" (Matt. 11:28).

His real name was Joseph. But the disciples called him Barnabas, and with good reason. His new name means "Son of Encouragement" (Acts 4:36). He provides a refreshing example for all of us.

He was sent to Antioch to observe what God was doing there. "When he arrived and saw the evidence of the grace of God, he was glad and encouraged them all to remain true to the Lord with all their hearts" (Acts 11:23). Later, he strongly affirmed Paul at a time when the disciples were hesitant to accept him (Gal. 2:1, 9). That's our man.

Some years back I could have used his support. The small Christian college where I served as an administrator changed presidents. I was demoted. Barnabas, where were you?

My friends were at a loss for words. Trite words of encouragement might have intensified my grief.

They decided to have a party for me. Everyone came beautifully dressed. Food was plentiful and delicious. But words still came hard. There were a few tears. The atmosphere was tense.

All of a sudden, one of my colleagues decided to break the ice. In a voice that could be heard by all, he declared, "I don't know about you guys, but this is the first time in my life I've attended a demotion party!"

That did it. Everyone cracked up in convulsive laughter. The party instantly became enjoyable. And from that moment on, I felt encouraged.

Paul puts it straight in Ephesians 4:29:

> Do not let any unwholesome talk come out of your mouths, but only what is helpful for building others up according to their needs, that it may benefit those who listen.

May we all remember the importance of committing ourselves to building up others.

But there is one more essential material for our bridges.

Consider Change Your Friend: Commitment to Flexibility

My father used to say, "Son, a rut is nothing but a grave with both ends kicked out." Saying it another way, Woody Allen once remarked, "A relationship is like a shark; it must constantly move forward or it dies."

Inflexibility is an enemy of healthy, Christian bridge building. Entrenchment, as the term implies, provides the mental image of wall construction.

Some of us are more prone than others to resist change—perhaps the powerful, the wealthy, those who live away from a large city. Also, those who are older.

Speaking of our senior citizens, I came upon this prayer the other day. It reveals a recognition of this pull toward inflexibility, and asks the Lord for grace:

> Lord, Thou knowest I am growing older. Keep me from being talkative and possessed with the idea that I must express my self on every subject. Release me from the craving to straighten out everyone's affairs. Keep my mind free from recital of endless details. Give me wings to get to the point.
>
> Seal my lips when I am inclined to tell of my aches and pains. They increase with the years and my love to speak of them grows sweeter with time. Teach me the glorious lesson that occasionally I may be wrong. Make me thoughtful but not nosey, helpful but not bossy. With my

vast store of wisdom and experience, it does seem a pity not to use it all, but Thou knowest, Lord, I want a few friends at the end.[4]

But, again, older people aren't the only ones who become set in their ways. Not by a long shot. As a university professor and counselor, I meet inflexible people of all ages.

I had to laugh to myself as my friend told the story. Also a professor at a Bible college, he related an incident that sounded all too familiar.

It was term-paper deadline time. One of his students stumbled in with a long and somber face. The touching story began. It seemed as though his wife was in the last weeks of pregnancy. He felt that the Lord wanted him to drop everything, including the trivial term paper responsibility, and unite with her in enjoying the birthing process.

Now, my friend has a reputation for being very hardnosed when it comes to making such concessions. But, somehow, this student had plucked a responsive chord in his heart. He agreed to setting back the due date, but only if the entire class could have the same favor.

He announced this concession at the next class session. Some students were upset. They had sacrificed to complete their project on time. Why encourage procrastination? Nevertheless, my teacher friend hung tough. It was high time that he showed himself to be more flexible, understanding, and compassionate.

Well, all the papers came in on the extended date—including that of the new father. The grading began. As the prof read through the masterpieces, one stood out for depth of thought and verbal sophistication. He glanced up at the name and it was, wouldn't you know it, the student he had made the concession for.

4. Entitled "cook's prayer," unpublished prayer contained in the news sheet "News From Oakie Acre," Fairfax, Virginia.

He thought, "This paper is so good that it could be published!" He couldn't help himself, he had to read it through again. It was then that he discovered the unvarnished truth: The paper had already been published! He recognized it, and went to the very source the student had copied.

The day of reckoning came. The poor fellow was summoned to his office. My friend began by complimenting him on the high quality of his work. The student beamed, saying that he was not surprised. He always knew that he had the potential. The professor could stand it no longer, and he confronted the young man with the evidence. He readily confessed and pleaded for mercy.

Knowing this professor as I do, I'm certain that the contrite plagiarist suffered the consequences.

The point is this. He had requested the professor to be flexible. Nevertheless, he had remained inflexible himself—as he held tenaciously to his undisciplined, irresponsible ways.

Once again, flexibility is essential in bridging to others. We must adapt to their thoughts, words, and actions until we arrive at a place of mutual respect.

And when we finally arrive at a communion of spirit, the assignment is not complete. Why? Because we grow at different rates. Therefore, we are forced to make many midcourse corrections with those we relate to. Never can (or should) we force them into our molds.

When we are flexible toward persons, we are showing them great respect. Also, we are revealing the depth of our own character.

Where from Here?

We have a clear and spectacular model for bridge building in Jesus Christ, our Lord. And his trustworthy blueprint reveals the precise specifications for following in his footsteps. Finally, we have the needed materials for construction within our grasp: commitment to time, risk, affirmation and flexibility. All we need is right here. Now it's time to go to work. To roll up our sleeves and, with his help, to begin our challenging and rewarding task. Let's get going.

No longer will violence be heard in your land, nor ruin or destruction within your borders, but you will call your walls Salvation and your gates Praise.—Isaiah 60:18

Stone walls do not a prison make,
Nor iron bars a cage.
                —Richard Lovelace "Lucasta. To Althea:
                From Prison"

The worst thing about crossing a bridge before you come to it is that it leaves you on this side of the river.—Old Proverb

4

Our Dedication to Labor

Recently, I spoke at a retreat in a beautiful, rustic monastery overlooking the Santa Barbara Channel. When arriving at the cell where I would be sleeping, I noticed this name over the entrance: St. Julian of Norwich.

Being inquisitive, I asked the monk to tell me about the life of this saint. He complied with enthusiasm.

It seems that Saint Julian lived in a small English town in the Middle Ages. While he was still very young, his church deemed him exemplary on all counts and decided to give him the ultimate recognition.

The day was announced, and everyone was there for the elaborate investiture ceremony. Singing was vibrant. Prayers were fervent. Praise to God for this saintly man was given.

Then it happened, just as everyone had expected. Saint

Julian was literally sealed into a small room that adjoined the cathedral. The walls were enclosed around him tightly, with only a small hole in the side. In that small, dark cubicle he would spend the rest of his life praying, administering blessings to passersby, and writing holy literature.

I thought to myself, "What a pity! Poor guy. That's worse than we treat our zoo animals today!" But wait. He wasn't the last good person to have sealed himself behind church walls. The church world is saturated with Saint Julians! And this reality strongly contributes to the fact that so few of us are building bridges to non-Christians.

Number Crunchers, We Hear You!

I've never been very impressed by statisticians, whom someone defined as "people who say that, if you put your feet in the oven and your head in the refrigerator, the middle of you will be the right temperature."

First, statisticians scare me. They tell me I don't have a chance. If I'm fortunate enough to escape drunk drivers and drug-crazed murderers, the disappearance of the ozone layer is sure to get me.

Second, the number crunchers insist on comparing me with something as uncomplimentary as a rat or monkey. They recently did this in their unsuccessful attempt to stop me from drinking diet soft drinks.

One more thing about the numbers guys. They twist statistics to support some pretty bizarre conclusions. I heard about one who used impressive figures relating human to stork populations in Europe, proof positive that storks really do bring babies. Now really!

But in spite of these misgivings, I must admit that one statistician recently got to me. His study found that only one in four hundred of us who claim to follow the master bridge builder is successful in linking someone to him each year. Think about that a moment. That's only one fourth of one percent.[1]

In our hearts, we realize that Jesus died so that such persons "shall not perish but have eternal life" (John 3:16). Furthermore, we know that he does not discriminate in his invitation, but desires that "all men [will] be saved and [will] come to a knowledge of the truth." (1 Tim. 2:4).

Unfortunately, our knowledge of this truth doesn't always spur us to action. Some of us remain apathetic, which the poet Thoreau describes as a state of "quiet desperation." Others of us labor, but hide behind thick walls. Encased. Entombed.

Is it not time that we who claim to be Christ's redeemed servants begin cutting yellow ribbons on scores of new bridges that will link us and our Savior with our desperately pagan world?

That means plenty of diligent and dedicated labor. Labor that is likely to tire us and maybe even make us look older. But is that really so bad?

Concerning our appearance, author Reuben Welch asks, "Shouldn't a Christian who has lived half a life look half used up? What are we saving ourselves for? To look good in our caskets?"

I say, Let's pull out all the stops. Let's jump into the thick of this God-ordained construction project. With rolled-up sleeves, let's use his model, blueprint, and essential materials to build bridges for him.

Our work assignment is divided into two important tasks. The first focuses on the initial construction, the second on maintenance. Both are challenging assignments.

1. Stated in Jon Johnston, *Christian Excellence: Alternative to Success* (Grand Rapids, MI: Baker Book House, 1985), p. 128.

Task Number One:
Building Reliable, Functional Structures

A man walked up to a workman who was digging trenches in New York City. After getting his attention, he asked, "Sir, what are you doing there?"

The laborer snapped back, "I'm making five bucks an hour!"

To satisfy his curiosity, the fellow went up to another ditch digger and asked the same question. The answer was much different. "I'm participating in the construction of a very impressive skyscraper."

Both were doing the same activity, but that is where their similarity stopped. The first was short sighted; the second visualized the great significance of his work.

We must see that the relationships our Lord helps us to build have eternal significance. Why? Because relationships have a crucial bearing on why most people affiliate with a church and become disciples of Jesus.

Win Arn says so, and he has plenty of support for his conclusion. In his scientific investigation, he found that 75–90 percent of all churchgoers identify a "relational factor" as being responsible for their attending.

Either a friend, relative, or neighbor networked them into the church body.

Another study found that 71 percent of all active church members today had responded to a "relational approach" to evangelism. This is contrasted with only thirteen percent who were drawn in by a content-oriented presentation of the Gospel.[2]

2. Quoted in "The Win Arn Growth Report: A Newsletter for the Leaders of Growing Churches," Number 15, Institute for American Church Growth, 709 East Colorado Boulevard, Suite 150, Pasadena, CA 91101, pp. 2–3.

For an enlarged discussion of this study and the application of the network principle of church growth, see the book *The Master's Plan for* Making Disciples, by Win Arn.

The author accentuates a concept made popular by Bible translators—dynamic equivalence. We must locate concepts that are dynamically equivalent in our culture today, that are relevant to both the secular world and God's Word. Then we can meaningfully translate biblical truth.

The bridge of content, whether constructed of lessons or sermons, is ineffective. Especially when unsupported by relationships.

So, fellow builders, as we establish links with others, we must be encouraged by the tremendous significance of our labor. We're doing more than depositing an hourly wage in the bank of heaven. Much more.

Seeing our work from this perspective should give us *inspiration.* Now we are ready for *perspiration* as we work at some very important tasks.

1. Personality Under Construction

In order to become skilled workmen we must allow Jesus to help us remove the rough edges from our personalities.

Whether by accident or intention, some of us are turnoffs. And the more we alienate others, the less we seem to be aware of the fact! As a result, people avoid us like porcupines, skunks, and growling dogs.

In what specific ways do we turn off others? Allow me to describe these three.

First, some of us are oblivious. We're so much into our own worlds that we don't have the foggiest notion about what is going on around us.

At Pepperdine University where I teach, 20 percent of our student body is from outside the United States. Of this number, many come from Third World nations where poverty is rampant.

By contrast, the students from these areas are typically very wealthy themselves. Their parents are, in fact, among the richest people in the world.

Recently, I was talking with a fellow who fit this cate-

In searching for these connecting bridges we must investigate the predispositions of Americans. How? By focusing on the content that is disseminated by the media.

Social scientists are saying that the predominant concerns today are friendship, love, and relationships. Perhaps that is why the great majority of Christians come to Christ and their church through social connections. They are, in effect, the dynamic equivalent of our culture on which we can build an effective evangelism strategy.

gory. He was from India. Without attempting to put him on the spot, I asked him about his concern for the destitute of his country.

Did the tens of thousands who anguished on the streets concern him? Did he lie awake at night worrying about their welfare? Did his heart ache when he saw the garbage trucks pick up the emaciated bodies of those who had starved?

Now, keep in mind that I was asking these questions of a well-mannered, responsible young man, whose smile lit up his entire face.

That's why I was surprised by his nonchalant answer. "No, prof, to be perfectly honest, I've never been concerned at all. I've never really seen those people."

In the same way, some of us have conditioned ourselves to avoid seeing. Or feeling. Or caring. Although we may not be isolated from those others, we've somehow insulated ourselves from them.

Jesus asks us to remove the scales from our eyes. To be truly sensitive to those around us, especially to those in need.

Second, more than a few of us are obnoxious. People can't stand to be around us. At best we're only tolerated.

We talk too much, or invariably say the wrong things. I'm reminded of a prayer that my mother shared. One that we're all well-advised to pray: "Lord, fill my mouth with worthwhile stuff, and nudge me when I've said enough."

Some of us have a well-rehearsed reservoir of annoying habits. We eat with our mouths open, chew on our fingernails, doze off during the pastor's message, have perpetual "doggie breath."

If only we could see ourselves as others see us. Perhaps then we would cease being so offensive and unappealing.

Third, a great number of us are ostentatious, always performing, forever on display in order to impress.

Matthew's Gospel declares, "Whoever humbles himself like [a] child is the greatest in the kingdom of heaven" (18:4). Similarly, James 4:6 says, "God opposes the proud but gives grace to the humble." Finally, the apostle whom Jesus called the rock admonishes, "Clothe yourselves with humility toward one another" (1 Peter 5:5).

Our Lord is unimpressed by our parading. So are other people.

These three o's—oblivious, obnoxious, ostentatious— must be eradicated from our personality no matter how deeply rooted they are.

2. An Inch at a Time

Bridge building requires more than placing six or eight massive beams across a river, along with a few side rails. Instead, there are millions of tiny parts—swivels, bolts, screws, metal slats. A good bridge is built by workers persistently connecting these small parts in a skillful manner.

Christian bridge construction must be just as deliberate and painstaking, done bit by bit with small acts of kindness and thoughtfulness.

I'm reminded of an incident that takes place regularly on a Philadelphia toll bridge. My friend, Anthony Campolo, crosses this bridge often.

If you have heard him speak or have read his books, you won't be surprised by a small act of kindness that he frequently renders.

When he pulls up to the collection booth to pay his toll, he invariably pays for the car behind him. It brings a little ray of sunshine to the other driver, raising by a fraction his confidence in mankind.

As he pulls away, Tony particularly enjoys seeing the toll receiver explain what has occurred to the recipient. It is a major production.

My point is this: We do our most effective bridge building in small increments, little acts of kindness, natural outgrowths of our love for Jesus and those for whom he died. With no glory or expected return.

Though seemingly insignificant, such acts combine to have a powerful effect, like the tiny snowflakes that melt together to form gushing mountain streams.

Bonaro Overstreet restates this important principle in verse:

> You say the little efforts that I make will do no good:
> They never will prevail; to tip the hovering scales,
>   where justice hangs in balance.
> I don't think I ever thought they would.
> But I am prejudiced beyond debate, in favor of my
>   right to choose which side will feel the stubborn
>   ounces of my weight.[3]

Jesus instructs us to not minimize our "ounces." Small gestures of kindness have great significance, even the giving of a cup of cold water.

> And if anyone gives even a cup of cold water to one of these little ones because he is my disciple, I tell you the truth, he will certainly not lose his reward (Matt. 10:42).

Relationships—the kind that are the most fulfilling and enduring—are constructed gradually. One smile here. A toll fee paid there. One sincere compliment here. A cup of cold water there. It all adds up. Not only that, it is multiplied by him just as the loaves and fishes were on two separate occasions.

Every morning we should ask, "What small gesture of kindness can I express to someone before this day is over?" In the Lord's eyes, it could be the most important event of the day.

Well, eventually the bridge is completed. The blueprints, tools, and excess materials are removed. In come the cleaners to make it shine. Bands, city officials, and crowds of onlookers gather to celebrate. Vehicles line up to be the first to cross.

---

3. Bonaro Overstreet, "Hands Laid Upon the Win" (source unknown).

We take a deep breath and say to ourselves, "At last, all of our labor is finished. We can enjoy what we have constructed forever. No more work!"

Right? Wrong. After building, we are only ready for the second essential task.

Task Number Two:
Maintaining the Bridges We Have Built

I must be naive. It seemed to me that after a bridge like the Golden Gate was completed and painted, that was that. Then someone clued me in.

An army of painters never stops painting. They start at one end, and continue until they reach the other end. Then they start over again. This has continued since the bridge's conception.

If they would stop their work, the salty ocean air would cause harmful corrosion. In a very short time the bridge would become unsafe as well as unattractive.

Like this paint crew, we must continually work at refurbishing and reinforcing the bridges we've built. Otherwise, they are likely to collapse. And this is true even for the bridges that we consider to be the most resilient. Allow me to illustrate.

I attended a Christian college on the West Coast. During those four years, some very sturdy bridges were built between me and my classmates. We were close. Even intimate. When we parted on graduation day, it seemed as though our bridges would remain firmly intact in spite of our separation.

Well, a few days ago Cherry and I attended my class reunion. It was an eerie feeling to walk into a roomful of strangers who were supposed to be close friends. We all had to wear name tags. Not only were names difficult to remember, but we looked much different.

What had occurred? To put it simply, we had neglected to maintain our bridges. Life's other priorities had intruded, causing us to relegate our relationships to the back burner.

Here's the good news. Our three-hour event was more than worthwhile. After becoming reacquainted, it was only a matter of minutes before we began to rekindle our relationships. As we laughed about old pranks (such as when "those other guys" somehow placed a sports car in the library) and requested prayers for special needs, we established a facsimile of old times. People relaxed. Communication became easy and fun. We had given the old bridges a fresh, new paint job.

Furthermore, we vowed to keep those brushes moving. Plans for a newsletter, notification of addresses, and another reunion are in the works. We realize now what it takes to keep even the closest relationships intact and growing.

What should we keep in mind while attempting to maintain and continually refurbish our relationships? I'd like to make a couple of suggestions.

Cultivate Contacts Consistently

We've all heard the adage, "Absence makes the heart grow fonder." That may be true for some people, or for most people during a short period of time. But in the long run, another common saying seems to be more accurate: "Out of sight, out of mind."

In sociology, we talk about a well-researched principle that concerns basic human nature. It is called the Homans thesis, after the person who formed and publicized it widely. In essence, it states: The more people interact under conditions of equality, the more they tend to like one another.[4] According to the researcher, the opposite is also true.

4. Refer to George C. Homans, *The Human Group* (New York: Harcourt, Brace, 1950), pp. 111–120; also discussed in Don Martindale, *The Nature and Types of Sociological Theory* (Boston: Houghton Mifflin Company, 1960), p. 480.

Establishing contacts with others can be enjoyable. Keeping them enjoyable is also very necessary if our relationships with them are to endure.

And when we approach this issue as Christians, there is still another important dimension. Our Lord expects us to take the time and go to the trouble of maintaining the relationships he has entrusted to us. That transcends the advice of George Homans, although it is consistent with it.

All of us have a particular sphere of influence. It includes immediate family members, work associates, neighbors, clerks, or anyone with whom we have or should have built a relationship. These are the people with whom we have an "in," more than with anyone else. When we speak, they listen.[5]

By making regular, caring contacts with them we are performing essential maintenance on important bridges. As a result, not only are our relationships with them strengthened, but so are those they have with one another and with our Lord.

Contacts can be made in many ways: In person. On the telephone. Through the mail.

My wife prefers the latter. She has committed herself to the task of writing approximately ten cards and letters each week. Usually they are targeted to persons who are sick, discouraged, lonely, or bereaved. In addition, she sends plenty to say "thank you" for kindnesses that have been extended to the Johnstons. It's her very own ministry—a way of keeping in touch. A way of bringing encouragement.

Her correspondence builds bridges, or lets others know

5. The Old Testament equates what we know as our sphere of influence with the Hebrew term that means "household," of which the several generations includes a family (Gen. 12:3 KJV). The New Testament uses the Greek term *oikos* to mean "household." Included in its meaning are friends, extended family, and associates. Win Arn says, "Bridges of *oikos* were used regularly as a means to a spread the Good News." After healing the demon-possessed man, Jesus instructed him to "go home to [his *oikos*] and tell them how much the Lord [had] done for [him]" (Mark 5:19). Following the ascension, *oikos*-evangelism caused the church to flourish. See Acts 16:15, 30–34.

that they are welcome to cross those we've already constructed. She lets others know that we care and are available for further contact.

Dean Martin used to close his television show with one statement: "Keep those cards and letters comin'." My admonition is similar: Keep those contacts comin'. Whether they are cards and letters, conversations, prayers, smiles, or telephone calls. They are absolutely essential for enhancing and strengthening relationships.

Always Advocate Acceptance

Tower Bridge in London is an impressive, beautiful structure. It would cost millions to build today. Nevertheless, in spite of its value, everyone is allowed to use it. Kids wearing soccer caps. Killers carrying weapons. Doctors rushing to help the sick. Drug addicts on their way to peddle destruction. The Tower Bridge is no respecter of persons.

In this sense, the structure is like our bridge to Jesus Christ. He accepts us, as Reuben Welch likes to say, *as* we are, *where* we are, *how* we are, right now! We need not shape up our act or take a crash course in righteousness in order to approach him. Rather, we can "come boldly unto the throne of grace, that we may obtain mercy, and find grace to help in time of need" (Heb. 4:16, KJV).

Like our Lord, we are to manifest an accepting spirit toward those with whom we have built relationships. This implies such things as

> listening intently to their concerns, while empathizing with their feelings;
>
> refusing to judge their behavior; and,
>
> allowing for their weaknesses, even if the latter overshadow their strengths.

All of this means somehow communicating to them: "It's okay to be you. I'll allow you as a divinely created son or daughter of God that freedom."

And what if even this kind of acceptance doesn't produce results in others? What if they refuse to cross the bridges we have constructed so skillfully and caringly?

In such cases our acceptance of them must remain intact. We must leave the structures standing and continue to maintain them, in hopes that such persons will someday choose to cross.

I know of a warm, Christian parent who invested unselfishly in a bridge to his son. Like the prodigal son, this lad refused to cross—or even to acknowledge—that the bridge existed. This was very discouraging to the parent. After having invested so much, his natural reaction was to dynamite that bridge so that the boy could never cross. Have you ever had that feeling toward someone?

Well, after much prayer and thought, my parent friend resisted this impetuous idea. With Christ's help, he vowed to leave the bridge intact.

Again, like the prodigal son, the young man came to his senses and "returned to his father's house." And when he did, he received complete acceptance. I wish this were the end of the story. Unfortunately, the boy had more lessons to learn and recrossed the same bridge to the old life.

But his father isn't about to give up. The bridge still stands and will continue to stand for the duration. My prediction is that eventually this errant fellow will cross that bridge one final time. And he will be home to stay at last.

Acceptance also means letting go. Allowing others to make their own decisions, refusing to preach or lecture, to shame or scold. Simply letting go is described in this inspirational reading by Barbara Johnson.

To let go doesn't mean to stop caring; it means I can't do it for someone else.

To let go is not to cut myself off; it's the realization that I can't control another.

To let go is not to enable, but to allow learning from natural consequences.

To let go is to admit powerlessness, which means the outcome is not in my hands.

To let go is not to try to change or blame another; I can only change myself.

To let go is not to care for, but to care about.

To let go is not to fix, but to be supportive.

To let go is not to be protective; it is to permit another to face reality.[6]

Possessiveness and acceptance are like oil and water; they don't mix. Relinquishing control is essential to cultivating our relationships.

You might be saying to yourself, "This business of building relationships sounds like a lot of work." If so, you couldn't be more right. Work to build. Work to maintain. The important question for us all is: Are we ready to join in the labor? Furnished with Christ's example, presence, blueprints, and materials, will we show up at the work site?

Absolutely! For we realize that our labor of love is exceedingly worthwhile. Recalling Paul's words, our "labor in the Lord is not in vain" (1 Cor. 15:58). Similarly, the writer to the Hebrews declares, "God . . . will not forget your work and the love you have shown him as you have helped his people" (6:10).

What is the result of our labor? Sturdy, dependable, beautiful bridges that stand tall.

But, building such impressive structures is not enough. There is another important consideration—that of destination.

It would be foolish to build a bridge beside, rather than across, a river, or to construct it to extend back to its point of origin, thereby making a continuous U turn.

---

6. Barbara Johnson, "Letting Go," source unknown.

Rather, these structures must be aligned with the banks. To places where people want and need to go.

Likewise, our relationship bridges must extend to a variety of important destinations. They must reach over chasms and gaps in order to establish linkage with a wide range of people. In that sense, they must be holistic and inclusive, rather than parochial and restricted.

In the section that follows, we shall closely examine the four kinds of essential destinations to which our bridges must extend.

Part 2

Bridges/Destination
Wholistic Relationships

Friendship is the inexpressible comfort of feeling safe with a person, having neither to weigh thoughts nor measure words.—George Eliot

No man ever went to heaven alone; he must either find friends or make them.—John Wesley

Friendship is like money, easier made than kept.
—Samuel Butler

5

Footbridges to the Devoted

Historians inform us of an experiment that was performed by Emperor Frederick II of Prussia. It was his contention that every newborn child possesses an intuitive knowledge of Latin, "the language of the gods."

To offer proof of his bizarre notion, he isolated a large number of infants. The only human contact permitted them was during their feeding, which was done without a word spoken.

Frederick just knew that after a few months all of the babies would spontaneously speak a beautiful, untainted Latin.

Results? You guessed it. The infants began to die, until only a few remained alive, and these few had irreparable brain damage. Not one, at any time during the experiment, uttered a single syllable of Latin!

Why had the experiment failed? Because the emperor's theory was ludicrous. Why did the babies perish? Because they were deprived of necessary, nurturing relationships during these crucial, formative days.

We might have expected such a tragic ending. After all, these were newborn infants. But most of us are adults. Are we, too, dependent on nurturing contacts with others? Absolutely.

We all have a desperate need to hear comforting voices. To feel the warm touch of others. To sense their uplifting spirits of camaraderie. In short, we need to receive and give "strokes."

Of course, the main suppliers of such life-sustaining support are those who are devoted to us—our friends, family members, work associates, leisure-time cronies, or church companions.

These are the people who are up close, the first people with whom we need to build bridges.

I cannot help thinking of the small, arched, decorative footbridges I saw in Japan. In a garden there were as many as a dozen, punctuating the sculptured landscape with beauty and grace.

We all need to build footbridges that link us in true friendship with people near to us.

Let's take a closer look at the dynamics of friendship.

The True Blue Few

On the wall of the photocopier room at our university, there is a sign that reads:

> A friend is one who—
>   *knows* you as you are,
>   *understands* where you've been,
>   *accepts* who you have become,
>   and still gently *invites* you to grow.

Such persons are rare. It was Abraham Lincoln who said if we have but one true friend, we should consider ourselves wealthy.

Recently, a plethora of books on friendship has appeared. Some are best sellers. Their message is consistent: Meaningful human existence is impossible without friendship ties.

So what else is new? Of course, friends are valuable. But can we lump all we call by this term in the same bundle? Author Jerry White doesn't think so. His classification provides helpful clarification.[1]

Levels of Intimacy

Level 1 acquaintances

Level 2 casual friends

Level 3 close friends
  a) associate
  b) personal
  c) mentor

Level 4 intimate friends

Acquaintances are those ever-changing relationships that we form in the course of daily living. People we recognize, and smile or say hello to in the market. Those we interact with as they serve us, such dentists and gasoline station attendants. According to White, we are involved with 500 to 2,500 acquaintances each year.

Acquaintances constitute the pool from which we choose casual friends. These are persons we see somewhat regularly, know on a first-name basis, and meet socially on occasion. They number from twenty to one hundred, and their friendships may last from a few months to a lifetime.

Though important for social and economic reasons, casual friendships rarely satisfy our innermost social needs. They tend to be too oriented toward personal gain, and are thus too superficial.

---

1. See Jerry and Mary White, *Friends and Friendship: The Secrets of Drawing Closer* (Colorado Springs: Navpress, 1982), p. 30f.

But, some casual friends become close friends, who can be of three kinds:

1. associate friends: ones who emerge from mutual participation (example: those involved in a Bible study with us)
2. personal friends: ones who remain close, regardless of time lapse or distance (example: sorority sisters)
3. mentor friends: ones who have guided or taught us (example: former professor or counselor)

We have from ten to thirty active close friends, and about the same number of inactive (persons we're separated from). Concerning the inactives, it's amazing how quickly it becomes just like old times again when we see each other, no matter how long we've been apart.

A few of our close friends trickle into intimate friendships with us. Most of us have no more than four, due to the fact that they consume so much of our time, energy, and concern.[2]

To these persons we bare our souls and share our deepest needs and hopes. We enjoy their presence immensely, even when they criticize us.

In fact, some of us seek their sometimes painful analysis of our ideas and performance. We feel that they've earned the right to "fire away." Also, we know that they will be honest and have our best interests at heart. Furthermore, they're likely to be open to our critique of them.

We all need buddies. Best friends who are available when we need them and with whom we can have helpful and healthy interchange.

In summary, most of us relate to people on these four levels of intimacy, with the result that we receive and

2. Ibid.

give varying degrees of companionship, trust, and acceptance.[3]

But Christians' friendships provide another benefit. They draw us closer to the master. Our linkages with brothers and sisters in Christ help us to do such things as resist temptation, maintain spiritual perspective, be accountable, and receive encouragement and uplift.

Jesus generously supplies us with "spiritual kin" who possess compassionate hearts. Because he lives within us, we have a unity that surpasses anything this world can exhibit. An authentic, Christ-centered fellowship. The kind that makes our lives a fulfilling ministry.

But some of us are saying, "That certainly doesn't describe the people at my church. They are pretty vicious."

Granted. What we have portrayed is the biblical ideal. It is true that church environments can become war zones rather than havens of tranquility. Why is this so?

Doves or Bantam Roosters?

dove (duv), n.: bird resembling small pigeon; symbol of peace and gentleness; person who advocates peace.

---

3. According to the Bible, friends bring out the best in us. Specifically, they do this by providing us with: (1) emotional encouragement. "Perfume and incense bring joy to the heart, and the pleasantness of one's friend springs from his earnest counsel" (Prov. 27:9). (2) help in trouble. "A friend loves at all times, and a brother is born for adversity" (Prov. 17:17). (3) personal stability. Without friends we are rootless for they keep us from self-centered wanderings and rash decisions. (4) spiritual help and counsel. "As iron sharpens iron, so one man sharpens another" (Prov. 27:17). (5) freedom of expression. Friends encourage us to speak openly and freely without fear of being condemned, even if our ideas lack a logical basis. (6) protection from isolation. Without friends we turn inward as we grow older. With friends, we're forced to communicate, to be committed, and to be held accountable. (7) love and acceptance. We need to be loved for who we are, not just wanted for what we do or might do. "Faithful are the wounds of a friend; profuse are the kisses of an enemy" (Prov. 27:6, RSV). (8) opportunities to give. To be a friend to our friends, we must contribute. And that meets another basic need of our lives.

Ibid, pp. 33–42; 45–47. Also, on p. 30 the author portrays the constituent parts of the arch of friendship: (1) foundation: personal relationship with Jesus Christ (2) supporting columns: time and effort (3) connecting stones in arch: love, deep sharing, self-sacrifices, encouragement, stimulation, spiritual challenge, loyalty, and fun.

See also Alan Loy McGinnis, *The Friendship Factor: How to Get Closer to the People You Care For* (Minneapolis: Augsburg Publishing House, 1979).

bantam (ban'tom), n.: chicken of a very small size; small quarrelsome person.[4]

Most of us think of God's house as a retreat where we can come to find rest for our souls. People there are peaceful—a virtual nest of doves.

But, as admitted above, churches can become battlegrounds. People can engage in such warfare as refusing to speak, indulging in slander, giving backhanded compliments, and threatening legal action.

Often such childish behavior results in church splits (or prunings). One rapidly growing denomination attributes its expansion to this fight-split-begin-new-church pattern. Not exactly the New Testament ideal!

The question is "Why?" Why do such attitudes and behaviors surface in the hallowed precincts of our churches?

Our situation may not be as bad as it seems, especially when compared with secular institutions. It just *seems* worse for two reasons.

1. Nonchurch people expect more from us who make great claims. They squint their eyes to locate any flaw. When found, it is blown out of proportion so they can say, "See there, we're really not so bad in comparison."

2. In addition, we expect and demand more from one another than outsiders do. As a result, we're quick to condemn our brothers and sisters when they manifest the slightest weakness.

Now, the first of these is self-explanatory. But concerning the second, allow me to elaborate.

When we become Christians, we become truly new. 2 Corinthians 5:17 (KJV) says, "All things are become

4. *The Random House Dictionary*, ed. Jeff Stein (New York: Ballantine Books, 1980), "bantam," p. 69; "dove," p. 273.

new." In what ways do we become new? And how exactly, do these newnesses affect our relationships with one another?

First, we have a new aim. Prior to becoming Christians, we desired to fit into and conform with our world. Our invisible antennas constantly tested the winds of opinion. Once we determined what "they" were doing and thinking, sheeplike we marched in the same direction.

After receiving Jesus into our hearts, our primary intent is to please him rather than men. We manifest a new independence from the reactions of others.

Unfortunately, the pendulum can swing too far. We can begin to disregard what our Christian brothers and sisters think. We can become very insensitive. Our attitude can become "Let the chips fall where they may. I answer only to God."

We must learn to be nonabrasive. Hebrews 12:14 says, "Make every effort to live in peace with all men."

Second, as new Christians we have a new kinship. And with that comes certain new rights.

If we are not careful, our new rights can prompt us to become presumptive, to take others for granted.

I can't help thinking about how inconsiderate we often become toward members of our biological families, doing things like turning the bathroom into a virtual swamp after showers, failing to put gasoline in the car for the next driver, or neglecting to wipe off the catsup bottle. It's these little things than can make home life pretty trying at times!

We often become inconsiderate toward our spiritual families, too. We phone in the middle of the night, drop by unannounced, request their sacrificial assistance. Or, in the church setting we do such things as whisper and write notes during the sermon, sing too loudly, throw down our bulletin in the parking lot, dominate Sunday school class discussion.

To these obnoxious facts of commission we add equally offensive acts of omission. We neglect to say thank you, refuse to answer an RSVP for a class social, fail to make a necessary hospital call.

Never should we allow ourselves to use or presume upon the lives of others, regardless of how close we feel toward them.

Third, when the newness of Jesus enters our lives, we have a new love. *Agape* love. The kind that is unconditional, sacrificial, and available to everyone. This God-sent love fills our being, and we begin to feel a closeness with others that we have never felt before.

This kind of love can make us very courageous and honest. Like so many things, that can be both good and bad. Good when courage and honesty make us open and transparent. Bad when we can become extremely blunt with one another. In fact, we can become brutally frank— which is only permissible for brutes!

However, we must be candid with one another. The writer of Proverbs says, "Faithful *are* the wounds of a friend." Better are they, says this ancient sage, than the kiss of an enemy (27:6, KJV). Nevertheless, we must learn to express honesty at appropriate times and in a sensitive, caring manner.

It is most ideal to bare our hearts to Christian friends whom we have known for some time, have mutual confidence with, and who have requested our honest reaction.

Otherwise, our advice is likely to come across as preaching, lecturing, or shaming. And these often produce feelings of guilt and resentment.

Finally, when Jesus becomes our Lord, we become subject to a new law—the law of right.

While unconverted we conformed to the laws of self-interest and pleasure seeking. This made us in many ways a law unto ourselves.

But now things are different. We strive to be guided by the principle of rightness. To paraphrase a statement made by John Gray, no longer do we do what others consider to be great; we do what we consider to be right!

However, like the other forms of newness described above, this one can be pushed to the extreme. We can develop a detective complex: Here we go, Christian Sherlock Holmeses, setting out to preserve the faith by rooting out all heresy.

This approach can become very hurtful. It is obvious that our quest for rightness must be tempered with godly wisdom and love. We are ill-advised to become judge and jury for all Christendom.[5]

To summarize, as humble followers of Christ we must cautiously accept our newness in him with gratitude.

But in so doing we must always remember to not become too independent, to not presume on the rights of others, to not exhibit brutal frankness, and to not play detective. Our prayer must be the same as Earl Lee's: "Lord, please help me to be tolerant without being compromising. Obedient without being judgmental. And honest without being unkind."

The remedy for all of these potentially threatening maladies is to grow in grace, and a key way we mature through God's grace is by investigating his Word.

What, exactly does the Bible say about the friendship bridges that we should be building with God's people?

The World's Greatest Friendship Manual

The late comedian W. C. Fields was forced to enter the hospital because of health problems. A visitor entered his room and caught him reading a Bible. Surprised, he asked, "W. C., what are you up to? Why are you reading *that* book?"

The rotund comic shot back, "I'm just looking for loopholes!"

In exploring what the Word says about equipping ourselves for friendship, we must not search for loopholes.

5. Taken from lecture notes of Dr. Richard Taylor. Class entitled "Doctrine of Holiness," 1966–67. Nazarene Theological Seminary.

Rather, we must be completely open to guidance. The Bible offers just that: clear, direct, understandable guidance.

What are some of the important things that God's Word tells us concerning our friendships?

Jesus: He's Numero Uno

While I was traveling through London's Hyde Park, our guide pointed to the cemetery and said, "Over there is a tombstone that reads, 'Love to my best friend, my adorable dog, who treated me far better than any of my five husbands.'"

Many dogs have been tagged with best-friend status. So have cats, horses, books, flowers, and even chocolates.

Nevertheless, as Christians we can assure ourselves of this fact: The lowly one from Galilee is, without a doubt, the best friend we can have. He's at the top of the list. That is why, with intense feeling, we sing:

> A friend of Jesus! Oh, what bliss.
> That one so vile as I.
> Should ever have a Friend like this.
> To lead me to the sky!
>
> (chorus)
> Friendship with Jesus! Fellowship divine!
> Oh, what blessed, sweet communion!
> Jesus is a Friend of mine.[6]

We don't refer to Jesus as our friend in a half-convinced or glib manner. Why? Because our claim is staked in Scripture.

The writer of Proverbs is right when he says, "There is a friend who sticks closer than a brother" (18:24). He has loved us through eternity.

In the fifteenth chapter of John's Gospel, our Lord illuminates the nature of our friendship with him.

---

6. "Friendship With Jesus," *Worship in Song* (Kansas City, MO: Lillenas Publishing Company, 1972), p. 204.

First, he shed his own blood for us. That is very significant, for, he says, "Greater love has no man than this, that he lay down his life for his friends" (v. 13).

Furthermore, he hand delivered to us the most intimate secrets of his Father. He declares, "I have called you friends, for everything that I learned from my Father I have made known to you" (v. 15).

Finally, he is straightforward in telling us how we can make our friendship with him complete. We must respond to him in complete obedience. He says, "You are my friends if you do what I command" (v. 14).

Make no mistake about it. The gift-wrapped package of friendship that Jesus delivers to our front door comes C.O.D. We're expected to pay the price, which is loving and faithful obedience (see John 14:21 and 15:10, 14).

In summary, we can have a fulfilling, abundant relationship with Jesus. He can be our closest friend. He has bridged us to God and has delivered to us his Father's commands and compassion. All we need to do is respond in obedience. And he even helps us to do that.

When Jesus truly becomes our friend, and we sense his unfathomable love and power, good things begin to happen.

For one thing, we begin seeing ourselves as someone beautiful. Why? Because we see ourselves through his eyes of love. And what do his eyes see when they look at us? Our potential for living a totally abundant life (see John 10:10)!

Here is another bonus. When we transcend the wall of just being chummy with Christ and really become his friend, we discover that we become more like him every day.

The same thing occurs with other humans with whom we are intimate. Psychologists tell us that we even begin to look alike. Facial muscle contractions are learned through imitation. In short, we learn to smile and frown like the persons we are close to. We take on their countenance as well as their ideas and attitudes.

The same thing occurs when we are close to the Savior. We begin to imitate him. What he is becomes an ever-increasing part of us. D. L. Moody, evangelist of yesteryear, put it so well: We may start our friendship with Jesus by emulating him, but as we grow closer, we will begin exemplifying him. And what a friend to exemplify!

Furthermore, our friendship with him has a dynamic, spill-over effect on our other friendships. We will begin to relate to others as he does to us, which is nothing but good.

It is to our other friendships that we now direct our attention.

Caution: Pseudo Friends at Large

Some time after Abraham Lincoln had become President, a reporter said to him, "Mr. President, your intimate childhood friends never really made anything of themselves. Some even became involved in serious trouble. With such unsavory early influences, how did you ever become President?"

Lincoln answered, "Sir, you are mistaken. These weren't my intimate friends. My closest friendships were made with Jesus Christ, Paul, Peter, Moses, and the other writers of the Bible."

Abe Lincoln chose his intimate friends carefully and wisely. So should we. Paul is emphatic when he cautions, "Do not be yoked together with unbelievers. For what do righteousness and wickedness have in common? Or what fellowship can light have with darkness" (2 Cor. 6:14)?

Scripture is telling us to avoid getting too close to persons who are not Christians, to maintain a certain measure of detachment (See 2 Corinthians 6:17–18). Certainly, avoiding courtship and marriage with them is implied. But, also, we must not be tempted to become intimately involved with them in business and leisure activities.

This may even mean burning some bridges with people we were close to prior to becoming Christians. Persons who are enslaved by a sinful lifestyle or intent on causing us to fall.

Question: If we're not supposed to be best friends with unbelievers, how can we hope to influence them to become believers? Answer: We can still meaningfully relate to such persons on a nonintimate basis.[7]

Recall the previous statement that most of us retain no more than four best friends. We are admonished to reserve those slots for Jesus and exemplary born-again Christians. Persons who will help us to grow spiritually.

Okay, it computes so far. We're to think of Jesus as our best friend, and we're well-advised to avoid becoming too close with unbelievers. But what about our Christian friends? How should we relate to them?

Our Hearts in Kindred Love

I can't help smiling to myself when hearing that contemporary Christian chorus, "Getting Used to the Family of God." We're stuck with each other. For now and for eternity. But that's not bad, for our Christian brothers and sisters are treasures of immense worth.

But this will come as no surprise: Our relationships with one another will not always be harmonious. We can truly love one another and still disagree. Paul and Barnabas did concerning whether John Mark should accompany them on their missionary journey (see Acts 15:37–40).

Our disagreements can and should eventually draw us closer together. Admittedly, this often takes time and patience.

Here's another observation. Although best friend status should be reserved for exemplary believers, all or most of our Christian friends won't be our best friends. We simply cannot accommodate that many.

---

7. We might refrain from doing the following with non-Christians: participate in their sinful activities, use their debase language, allow ourselves to become romantically linked with them. In attempting to reach out to sinners, often we carelessly slip into Satan's traps. Result: We become indistinguishable from those we are striving to convert.

But regardless of our degree of intimacy, as members of our Lord's family we must relate to each other in a loving and caring manner. Jesus says, "All men will know that you are my disciples, if you love one another" (John 13:35).

If we focus our attention on such love for one another, we will do two things:

Believe the best. In the Book of Titus we read, "To the pure, all things are pure" (1:15). Call it what you will—naivete, gullibility, fantasy—the fact remains that we must believe the best in our Christian brothers and sisters. That means that we'll always be willing to give one another the benefit of the doubt.

William Harley describes an invisible "love bank" that we all possess. As Christians, we continuously deposit loving actions into one another's accounts. A kind word. An earnest prayer. A needed gift. This giving occurs spontaneously as a result of Christ's presence within us.

The result is that love accumulates in our accounts. Thereafter, if we hear something that is suspicious or slanderous about one another, we draw from our stored-up reserves to cover it.[8] We say something such as, "Sorry, but I can't believe that about him. He's always been a loving and respectable person."

Of course, this does not imply that we will ignore well-documented negative evidence. It simply means that we'll be careful to not prematurely and unjustly judge.

Neglect to neglect! A few years ago a tragedy occurred along the Ohio River. The large, well-engineered bridge that links Ohio with West Virginia collapsed. Semi-trailer trucks, cars, motorcycles, and pedestrians were hurled into the deep, watery chasm below.

A thorough investigation discovered that the chief inspector had neglected to periodically examine essential parts of the structure.

8. See Willard Harley, *His Needs, Her Needs: How to Affair Proof Your Marriage* (Old Tappan, NJ: Fleming Revell, 1986).

No matter how strong our bridges, whether physical or relational, they will collapse if neglected.

We must never neglect the upkeep on our Christian friendship bridges. Periodic inspection tours will reveal weakness, decay, and stress points. Then we can promptly respond by making the necessary repairs. Continuous preventative maintenance is crucial.

Believe the best. Neglect to neglect. Both of these are essential ingredients in forming and building friendships. And never were they more evident than in the lives of David and Jonathan, as recorded in 1 Samuel 16–20.

From Goliath to Gilboa

Who could have predicted it? The son of a lowly sheepherder became the best friend of the son of Israel's king.

Except for their excellent battlefield skills, they had very little in common. In fact, they might have become bitter rivals for the throne.[9]

But, instead, they became "one in spirit" (with "knit" souls, KJV). Jonathan loved David "as himself."

They made a covenant, which made them "brothers" for life. To symbolize this, Jonathan gave David some impressive gifts. His princely robe and tunic (inner garment), implying that David was now part of the royal household. Also, he offered his sword (badge of his highest honor), bow and belt (containing his purse, secrets and sacred treasures). The latter, fittingly, gave David the countenance of a respected soldier.[10]

9. "None had so much reason to dislike David as Jonathan had, because he was to put him by the crown, yet no one regards him more." *The Bethany Parallel Commentary on the Old Testament* (Minneapolis: Bethany House Publishers, 1985), p. 545. Taken from the condensed edition of *Matthew Henry's Commentary on the Whole Bible in One Volume* (1960 by Marshall, Morgan and Scott, Ltd.; 1961 by Zondervan Publishing House).

10. "Such covenants of brotherhood are frequent in the East. They are ratified by certain ceremonies, and in presence of witnesses, so that the persons covenanting will be sworn brothers for life.

"To receive any part of the dress which had been worn by a sovereign, or his eldest son and heir, is deemed, in the East, the *highest* honor which can be conferred on a subject (see Esther 6:8)." Ibid. Taken from *The Jamieson, Fausset, and Brown Commentary.*

The shepherd from Bethlehem had really cashed in. But what led to this impressive pledge of oneness? Let's set the stage.

King Saul had grievously sinned, and Samuel had denounced his sovereignty. The prophet then anointed David to become Israel's next king.

While awaiting his ascendancy to the throne, David became resident palace harpist to the tormented king. The Word declares: "Whenever the [evil] spirit from God came upon Saul, David would take his harp and play. Then relief would come to Saul; he would feel better, and the evil spirit would leave him."

Soon came threats from the Philistines and their challenge for any Israelite to fight Goliath, who was over nine feet tall. (Can you imagine his salary in the NBA, if he were alive today?)

David was delivering roasted grain and bread to his brothers on the front line when he heard Goliath's defiant shouts. Also, he saw Israel's best soldiers run away "in great fear."

This distressed him greatly. Somehow he secured permission from the king to fight this bully. His weapon was a slingshot. His ammunition was five smooth stones. In the faceoff, David yelled out his testimony: "The battle is the LORD's."

Having to use only one-fifth of his ammunition, the lad felled the giant. Then the Philistines did some running themselves. David returned a hero and had an audience with King Saul. It was just after their discussion, overheard by Jonathan, that the two boys made their friendship covenant.

"Saul's [attire] would not fit him (David), but Jonathan's did. Their bodies were of a size, a circumstance which well agreed with the suitableness of their minds. David is seen in Jonathan's clothes, that all may take notice he is a Jonathan's second self. Our Lord has thus shown his love to us, that he stripped himself to clothe us, emptied himself to enrich us; nay, he did more than Jonathan, he clothed himself with our rags, whereas Jonathan did not put on David's." Ibid. Taken from the condensed edition of *Matthew Henry's Commentary.*

So here they were. Bonded. Intimate. Totally supportive. Committed. Just as best friends are supposed to be.

We might say to ourselves, "But their covenant was
made during a time of rejoicing. They both had stars in
their eyes. Friendships flourish at such times, when
things are going well.

Good point and usually the truth. The flip side of this
statement is that when times get tough, many friendships
crumble. Did this happen in the relationship between
David and Jonathan? In a word, no.

Saul became insanely jealous of David's popularity,
especially among the women. He twice hurled his spear at
David while he was giving a harp concert. The king offered Michal, his daughter, in marriage to the young
celebrity, but for a price. He must kill one hundred Philistines. Saul's idea was to have David himself slain in the
attempt.

Neither of these attempted murders worked. The agile
boy dodged the spears and successfully completed the
military mission. He married Michal, and Saul became
even more furious. Jonathan and all court attendants were
ordered to kill David.

Hearing this, Jonathan began doing the kinds of things
that all good friends should do.

First, he warned his friend of Saul's wrath.

Second, he defended David's integrity to his father. He
"spoke well of David to Saul."

Third, after Saul calmed down and agreed to cease his
vengeant pursuance of David, Jonathan bridged between
the attackee and the attacker. He "brought him [David] to
Saul."

Unfortunately, Saul set out on another rampage upon
hearing of David's additional battlefield successes. He
attempted to "pin him [David] to the wall with his spear."

So it was back to square one. David once again fled for
his life. After stopping off to see Michal and Samuel,
David met with Jonathan. He poured out his heart. Again,
Jonathan exemplified true friendship. He listened. He

offered hope. "You are not going to die!" And he expressed a willingness to help. "Whatever you want me to do, I'll do for you."

Well, the story goes on and intensifies. Like a bloodhound, Saul continued to pursue David. Jonathan just kept on being his friend, and their friendship deepened. They "wept together" and even pledged a bonding between their descendants.

Eventually, David was forced to hide behind Philistine lines. When Saul heard this, "he no longer searched for him." The chase was over. No doubt, David was relieved. But the Scriptures tell us no more about any contacts with Jonathan. The logistics may have made it impossible for them to get together.

Nevertheless, the friendship endured. How do we know? A final battle between the house of Saul and the Philistines occurred on Mount Gilboa. Saul and Jonathan were slain. David received the news. And as expected of a good friend, he grieved deeply.

The beautiful but sad lament is recorded in 2 Samuel 1:17–27. In this moving passage, David says,

> O mountains of Gilboa,
>   may you have neither dew nor rain,
>   nor fields that yield offerings of grain.
> For there the shield of the mighty was defiled. . . .
> I grieve for you, Jonathan my brother;
>   you were very dear to me (v. 21, 26).

Gilboa was cursed. I recently saw its rocky, barren surface. It stands there bleak and haunting.

Just as real was the intense grief that David felt for his fallen friend.

Nevertheless, he was left with many consoling memories. Memories of a friendship that was deep. And solid. And true. A friendship that stands tall as a model for our intimate relationships today.

We need friendships like David and Jonathan's. They enrich our lives as people. And as Christians.

But, we must do more than build friendship bridges. It is imperative that we establish linkage with those who do not desire us, even those who are defiant toward us. We will next explore this difficult but rewarding challenge.

I have resolved that no man shall ever lower me to the level of hatred.—Booker T. Washington

He that cannot forgive others breaks the bridge over which he must pass himself; for every man has need to be forgiven.—Lord Herbert

You know the honeymoon is over when your wife lets you lick the eggbeaters, but refuses to turn off the mixer.
—David Davenport

6

Drawbridges to the Defiant

At San Diego's Wild Animal Park, the following sign is posted at the entrance:

> **Please do not!!!!!!**
> annoy, torment, pester, plague, molest, worry, badger, harass, heckle, persecute, irk, bullyrag, vex, disquiet, grate, beset, bother, tease, nettle, tantalize or ruffle
> THE ANIMALS!

If we changed the last two words to "other people," the sign could appropriately be placed almost anywhere. On billboards. In magazines. Even in the narthexes of churches!

The simple truth is this: We're often bestial in the way we treat our fellow humans. Sometimes this is blatantly direct, but more often it is cleverly disguised.

If not the initiators of such abuse, we're likely to be the recipients of such harassment. We struggle through life. Cringing. Avoiding. Grieving.

Said another way, most of us either have interpersonal problems or we are the cause of such difficulties.

You guessed it. I'm about to suggest that we not engage in aggressive behavior, whether directly or indirectly. Paul says, "Let us therefore make every effort to do what leads to peace and to mutual edification" (Rom. 14:19).

That suggestion is probably much easier for us to comply with than my second one: We need to construct bridges to persons who defy, discourage, and even attempt to destroy us. A humorist described such people as being those who make us wish birth control could be made retroactive. Persons who serve only one useful purpose in life—to provide a terrible example. Ones who would gladly knife us in the back in order to have us arrested for concealing a weapon!

We mutter to ourselves, "Build bridges to these persons? Get serious. Who needs to be linked up with such clowns?" Answer: We do, if Jesus is our Savior.

Granted, being around such persons heightens the possibility of continual crises. But such crises need not devastate us. In the Chinese language, the word for crisis is *wei-ji*, and it has two meanings: danger and opportunity. With the Lord's help, we will focus on the second.

Excuse me, but would you help me lift this piece of steel? It's time we began building bridges to the defiant. By the way, don't expect these to be like the ornate footbridges we construct to friends. Rather, drawbridges are required, the kind the Crusaders built in the Middle Ages.

I stood on one such structure in Caesarea. It extended from the ancient castle over a deep moat. Our guide explained that it, like all drawbridges of that time, was built during an unstable, threatening period. It offered protection, for when raised, it functioned as a wall that restrained potential enemies.

A stationary bridge would have allowed invasion by providing complete access to the castle.

Again, bridges to the defiant must be drawbridges. And sometimes they must be raised. Interchange should be discontinued. Emotions are too high. Threat is too great. Things need to settle down. But, such bridges stand ready to be lowered the moment there is potential for productive and peaceful relationships.

But why must drawbridges be constructed to those in the church? How could *that* be a threatening environment?

Welcome to the Alligator Pond

As mentioned in the last chapter, even sincere and conscientious Christians can become abrasive. When they accept the new life in Christ but refuse to grow in grace, interpersonal problems can quickly develop. And when this occurs, shock waves are likely to be felt throughout the entire church body.

Unfortunately, as we all know, many church people fit this description. They're intentionally misery-makers. Human alligators. Who look threatening and behave viciously.

I prefer to term such persons "irregular people." That's better than calling them what some do: schizoids, paranoids, sickies, or weirdos.

Let's examine some of their telltale characteristics. And, perhaps, names and faces to surface in our minds.

First, irregulars usually have "selective blindness." They might be perfectly capable of seeing most people with flawless 20/20 vision. However, when peering at others, their eyesight is distorted.

One of their children might be targeted for unfair criticism, while the others are treated with great respect. Or they may unfairly criticize a Sunday school teacher, vocalist, or pastor for fictitious reasons.

When we're victims of such persons, we're at a severe disadvantage, for other people who are treated hospitably by our attacker just can't seem to empathize with our plight.

Second, in putting off and putting down certain people, irregular people make biased comparisons. They cite others who are smarter, richer, more talented or—worst of all—better. They make such comparisons in staccato regularity.

When confronted by these unfair contrasts we often panic. Some of us fight. Others of us flee. But most of us simply try harder to please.

Ironically, increased effort usually does little more than reinforce the irregular's negative stereotype of us. According to his twisted logic, our trying harder only substantiates the reality of our "problem."

I vividly recall an ordeal during my teen years. Our church youth leader seized every opportunity to make me feel badly about myself. His attempts fed into the pool of tremendous insecurities I already possessed.

In order to compensate, I began a rigorous self-improvement program. The increased effort brought results. But, my nemesis wasn't impressed in the least. In fact, he became even less receptive of me, and even refused to acknowledge my presence in public. The hurt was especially deep, because my father was the minister.

What I experienced is not unusual. Many of us have endured similar experiences. And the painful memories linger.

Third, irregular persons have a knack for possessing emotional deafness. They ebb and flow. Sometimes, they come across as open and sensitive. Then, with as much warning as a California earthquake, they become deaf to what we're saying and feeling. They pull away. Constrict. Become human walls.

It's then that we feel like screaming, "Why don't you hear me?" Also, we hear ourselves repeating messages to them over and over again. But to no avail. It isn't long before we see that we're no longer talking to living, breathing human beings. They've become stone masks.

Parent-teen conversations often take this unfortunate turn. So do discussions between persons who insist on voicing positions that they have received, warmed over, from family or friends. In both cases the result is impasse.

Fourth, irregulars almost always have serious communication problems. As someone remarked, "About the only time they open their mouths is to change feet!"

IPs love to select only the most inflammatory words from their vast arsenals. Not only that, they blurt out such verbal bullets at the most inappropriate moments.

Example. I served on a church board with someone who detested me. If I were on fire, I'm certain this person would gladly have contributed a can of gasoline.

We were interviewing a prospective senior pastor. Things were going well. The spirit was upbeat. Communication flowed. That is, until this person caught wind that I felt positive about the candidate.

Immediately, the jagged-edged questions were posed to the candidate. "Why do you have to leave the church you're from? Have you been asked to leave?" Questions that were obviously intended to put him on the defensive.

The hearts of the other board members sank in unison. The candidate stuttered a bit and then awkwardly attempted to rephrase the question. But it was futile. A tub of verbal ice water had been thrown in his face. He withdrew his name.

We've all been victimized by the misplaced, mistimed statements of aggressors. Persons who seem to have words for everything but an apology.

Fifth, irregular people are easily offended. Although they dish it out, they're unable to take it. Their oversensitivity is astounding. As someone mused, "Whenever a football team huddles, they're apt to think that the players are talking about them."

No doubt, their own aggressiveness provides irregulars with hypersensitivity. They continually fear that they might receive returns on their painful investments of ill will. Their victims are likely to retaliate.

This implies that IPs are very insecure, though most display a gruff exterior. The slightest criticisms from others cut them to the quick.

I recall knowing a church organist who was the epitome of irregularity. He demanded perfection, and targeted certain people for abuse. The latter were persons who might interfere with his Sunday performance. People shuddered in his presence.

One day our music committee met to brainstorm. A few minor improvements were suggested concerning his performance. Well, our friend came completely unglued at the hint that his area manifested any weaknesses.

Furthermore, he promptly took a walk. He wasn't about to stay around and receive such slanderous abuse. To his surprise, our church drew one big, corporate deep breath.[1]

Why are irregulars irregular? How do they arrive at that unfortunate condition?

Taxonomy of Troublemakers

Author Joyce Landorf offers a helpful classification of irregular people.

Regular Irregulars

She terms the first type "regular irregulars." These are persons who have had the misfortune of a deficient upbringing. Their parents were too restrictive or too passive, too miserly or too giving, too committed or too complacent. Somehow, there was a lack of balance.

Regular irregulars are usually not favorite children. They have sensed from earliest childhood that their parents consider them inferior. And they're reminded of this by continuous comparisons between themselves and their siblings or peers. They can shut their eyes and hear, "Why can't you be like_____?"

1. Joyce Landorf, *Irregular People* (Waco, TX: Word Books, 1982), Excerpted from Chapter 2, pp. 27–50.

This tragic form of child abuse has caused them to perpetually weep inside. And to manifest such counter-productive emotions as guilt, anger, and jealously.

Personality-defect Irregulars

The second classification is "personality-defect irregulars." These are persons who are serious misfits in society.

Such persons are everywhere, even on the campuses of universities. Students are often blunt in their assessment of such persons. Rejecting verbal subterfuge, they call them some pretty uncomplimentary names.

There are "flakes," who never follow through. Though making grandiose promises, they inevitably flake out, disappointing and infuriating all who have counted on them. Flakes do such things as stand up their dates and forget appointments with professors.

Then there are "nerds," who are awkward and absent-minded. As a result, they are unaware of others and live in their own worlds. They eat alone or with other nerds in the cafeteria, lurk around libraries or labs, and wear out-dated, unpressed clothes. Their hygiene approximates that of a camel's.

Finally, my students refer to "bozos," who are known for their glaring incompetencies. When physically un-coordinated, they are called "klutzes." Bozos match their incompetence with inconsideration. They do such things as never returning library books that the rest of the class needs, and insulting their professors by closing their note-book fifteen minutes before the end of the session.

We smile at their graphic university jargon while recalling similar persons we know. These people, again, have one thing in common: They're plagued with a crippling personality defect.[2]

2. Seen in *The Christian Reader*, in an article entitled "Bookshorts—Condensed from the Book: Irregular People," by Joyce Landorf, p. 103.

Sociopathic Irregulars

Here is a third classification: "sociopathic irregulars." Such individuals appear to have no feeling. They are as calculating as a tax accountant. As cold as a mortician. And it doesn't seem to bother them.

They appear to need no one's assistance. They're totally self-sufficient. At least, they like to think they are.

Nevertheless, these lone rangers know how to turn on the charm. In their detached manner they're able to demonstrate great social skills in public. And the unaware are greatly impressed.

I'm reminded of Stanley the cat, who lives next door. I've tried everything I know to relate to the little iceberg. Food. "Cat talk." But nothing has worked. The feline has remained his independent self.

That is, until my sister-in-law came to visit. She brought Tiger II (Tiger I was consumed by a California coyote).

The moment she let her animal out of the car, Stanley came running. Bright eyes. Polite meows. Playful roll-overs in the grass. Instant charm.

Incidentally, that was over a year ago. And since Tiger II left that day, Stanley has backslid into his former pattern. Such hypocritical behavior qualifies him to be classified as a sociopathic irregular—just like some people we all know.

Mental Irregulars

To these three types author Joyce Landorf adds a fourth: "mental irregulars." They have a form of mental illness due to genetic or stress-related causes. As a result, they are genuinely handicapped in their ability to relate in a healthy, positive manner.

Are there many of these persons in our world? Yes. It is estimated, for example, that over 60 percent of America's homeless fall into this category.

Do mental irregulars congregate in our churches? Affirmative. Why? Because there they feel most accepted. We should be honored to have them in our midst, for they provide us with an opportunity to serve Jesus. It was he who said, " . . . Whatever you [do] for one of the least of this brothers of mine, you [do] for me" (Matt. 25:40).

I admittedly have a soft spot in my heart for those whose mental deficiency is related to advanced aging. Problems associated with arteriosclerosis, which affects certain processes of the brain, are tragic indeed.

During the waning days of my father's life, I witnessed some of these difficulties. He began having small strokes, causing him to lose touch temporarily. He babbled. His mind wandered. He dozed off continuously. He even drove through red lights without seeing them.

But what concerned me most was his abrupt change in attitudes. He became caustic and reactive. Many things upset him greatly. I worried, and asked myself if Christians are supposed to manifest such attitudes, even in old age.

Anyone who knew Dad will tell you that he had always been upbeat and energetic. He was one to take control, to see the best in everyone and in every situation, no matter how bleak. That is why his stroke-plagued behavior was such a shock.

But after talking with a medical specialist, I understood what was occurring. It was quite normal for such a stroke syndrome to set in. The personality typically makes convulsive changes. Often for the worse.

Best of all, our Lord truly understands. So should we.

There we have four kinds of irregular people, all of whom can become very difficult for us to relate to, especially when we're close to them.

What approaches can we take? Are there any suggestions that might assist us? I believe that there are. Allow me to share a few.

The first group of tips focuses on our personal perspectives that can assist us in coping with these people. The second will zero in on specific strategies for relating to the defiant ones and irregulars.

Brushing Up Our Psyches

Difficult people are about as rare as air. They invade our jobs, shopping malls, marriages, and churches. Our particular interest is on the last of these.

But, before reflecting on irregulars that inhabit pews, let's turn our attention toward their victims. That's us. We need to be able to cope. And that has a lot to do with the perspective we choose.

Psychologist Harry Stack Sullivan refers to the need to "reframe life's" experiences, especially painful ones. The image is one of an old picture in a faded cardboard frame. It couldn't look more unappealing. But, when we place the same photograph inside a large, polished cherrywood frame, it looks like a masterpiece.

Similarly, we must take distasteful and discouraging events in our lives and put them in new "perception frames." We will then see the irregulars, who have heretofore haunted us, in a different and better light. Best of all, we'll be in control of—rather than victimized by—the perceptions of our experiences.

In creating the kinds of perceptions that will help us cope, we should keep in mind the following strategies.

First, we must put far more emphasis on the future, less on the present, and still less on the past. As Earl Lee likes to say, "It's straight ahead into life's tomorrows."

All too often we get bogged down in taking repeated "museum tours" into the past. We focus on past injustices. Past attacks. Past slights. And the longer we dwell on history's blows, the more resentful and depressed we're likely to become. Increasingly, we wish for revenge.

Again, the past must be shelved. When referring to it at all, we can rejoice in its rewards and be thankful for its valuable lessons.

In a very real sense, we should do a bit of romanticizing about past pains. I recall hearing about a lad whose father had been hung. When asked one day how his dad died, he replied, "My dad met his end when a platform on which he was standing in the town square suddenly collapsed." Now that's painting a rosy picture of a tragic event!

Paul encapsulates this principle in his admonition to the church at Philippi. "Forgetting what is behind and straining toward what is ahead, I press on toward the goal" (Phil. 3:13b).

Church leader J. B. Chapman stated it this way: "There are too many tomorrows for me to accept as final *any* slight, or defeat, or failure that may come today!"[3] I say, "Amen."

It's time to tear down the museums. To bury the hatchets. To lay to rest past grievances.

Second, we must exchange rigidity for flexibility. The Golden Gate Bridge was made to sway up to twenty-one feet in either direction. If not given that latitude, it would surely collapse when hit by the slightest ocean breeze.

Likewise, we must be willing to bend. The Apostle from Tarsus testifies, "I have become all things to all men so that by all possible means I might save some" (1 Cor. 9:22).

This means refusing to react in a defensive manner when irregular people insult us. Roy Angell, author of *Holiness Alive and Well*, admonishes us to "be a little kinder, a little sweeter, a little more giving. . . than anyone has a right to expect you to be!"[4]

What should we do when receiving unfair attacks? Pass them along to Jesus. We are only the middle persons. He desires to receive our burdens, no matter how heavy. Peter says, "Cast all your anxiety ["care," KJV] on him [Jesus] because he cares for you" (1 Peter 5:7).

When irregular persons see that they're not getting to us, they can lose their enthusiasm for launching assaults. But, whether they do or not, flexibility will help us to cope.

---

3. Bertha Munro, *Truth for Today* (Kansas City, MO: Beacon Hill Press, 1947), p. 338.

4. Roy Angell, as quoted by W. T. Purkiser in *Holiness Alive and Well* (Kansas City, MO: Beacon Hill Press, 1973), p. 40.

Third, we must be willing to reduce our level of expectation. Often we carry around a visual image of what people should become, as well as a timetable for this to occur.

Only our Lord knows what all of us should become. We are not omniscient and should refrain from judging each other. Joaquin Miller articulates this truth.

> In men, whom men condemn as ill,
> I find so much of goodness still.
> In men whom men pronounce divine,
> I find so much of sin and blot.
> I dare not draw a line between the two,
> where God has not.[5]

We're well advised to put away our measuring instruments and chisels, and allow God to change irregular persons as he wishes when he wishes.

Furthermore, we must patiently await his time for us to construct drawbridges to the defiant. Just as no engineer would advocate building while swollen flood waters race by, so we must bide our time. The writer to the Hebrews reveals the secret. "For [we] have need of patience . . ." (10:36, KJV).

How are these three goals accomplished? Through faithful and intense prayer. When our hearts become melted and obedient, our Savior will help us to envision a glorious tomorrow. He will make us flexible and provide the gift of patient endurance. And when he does, our coping will become a cinch.

But, it's not enough to sit back and cope. We must employ Bible-based strategies for interfacing with irregular persons. What are these strategies?

---

5. Joaquin Miller, "In Men Who Condemn." Transcribed from a sermon delivered by Lamar Kincaid, at Longboat Key Chapel, Longboat Key, FL, 1973.

Warning to Irregular People: Here We Come!

Strategy number one: We must forgive.

Even though we are the innocent recipients of wrong, the first move toward healing is always ours, and it consists of total forgiveness. Ephesians 4:31–32 reads:

> Get rid of all bitterness, rage and anger, brawling and slander, along with every form of malice. Be kind and compassionate to one another, forgiving each other, just as in Christ God forgave you.

Often our forgiving will also involve asking forgiveness. First from our heavenly Father, and second from those we have wronged or thought wrongly about. Our Lord provides the procedures for the latter in Matthew's Gospel.

1. "Remember that your brother has something against you" (5:23).

2. "Leave. . . and be reconciled to your brother" (5:24).

3. "Come and offer your gift [to God]" (5.24).

The key word is "reconciled." It means "to resolve or settle." Thus, when we're at fault or share in the blame, we must do our utmost to correct the situation. For some this seems like a giant, square pill to swallow. But with the Savior's guidance, it can be a meaningful act of supreme worship.

But how about when we're completely free of fault or guilt? When irregular people have sought to mangle our psyches? To use our hearts for target practice?

Again, we must rise above the temptation to become paralytically bitter. The kind of bitterness that expresses itself in statements such as, "I've been used and abused." "Everyone's against me." "I'm being neglected, forgotten, and overlooked." "Curse it all, I'd rather be dead!"

We must break through the threatening clouds of such defeat and into the brilliant sunlight of forgiveness. David Augsberger wisely instructs us to:

1. Forgive immediately after you feel the first hurt. With time comes resentment, and it is much cheaper to pardon than to resent. Forgive before the sting begins to swell and the molehill mushrooms into a mountain. Before bitterness sets in.

2. Forgive continually. People usually mature slowly. It's often two steps forward and one step backward. Focus on their direction rather than their rate of progress. Generously forgive, as Jesus said to Peter, "not seven times, but seventy-seven times" (Matt. 18:22b).

3. Forgive finally. Forgetful forgiveness is not "a case of holy amnesia which erases the past." It is the healing which extracts the poison from the wound. So that the memory is powerless to arouse us to anger.[6]

Forgiveness restores the present, helps the future, and helps us to release the past.[7] Again, its purpose is true reconciliation. Often that occurs. But frequently it does not. At times, those involved remain apart. The drawbridge remains slightly raised, enough to disallow the flow of interchange.

6. "Does Forgiving Take Time?" in *Building Self-Esteem*, ed. Gene Van Note (Kansas City, MO: Beacon Hill, 1983), pp. 46–54. Charles Swindoll quotes Amy Carmichael's helpful statement on the need to forget: "If I say, 'Yes, I forgive, but I cannot forget,' as though the God, who twice a day washes all the sands on all the shores of all the world, could not wash such memories from my mind, then I know nothing of Calvary love." Charles R. Swindoll, *Improving Your Serve: The Art of Unselfish Living* (Waco, TX: Word Books, 1981), p. 68.

7. Author Lewis Smedes addressed Pepperdine University faculty on the subject of forgiveness. He offered these timely insights: (1) Forgiveness doesn't mean tolerating past pain, forgetting instantaneously, or excusing the offender. (2) The reasons for forgiving are: (a) The hurting of the once offended will not continue. (b) God has forgiven, and requires all offended who bear his name to forgive. (c) Forgiving releases the offended from feeling that God loves the offender less because of anything he has done or might do. (d) The principle of forgiveness makes for a better world. Ghandi: "If everyone lived by the eye-for-an-eye premise, the whole world would be blind." (3) Red Flags! (a) Don't impose forgiveness as a moral duty. Few forgive because of this reason; rather, they do so because failure to forgive causes them great misery. (b) Don't demand that people forgive too fast. It wasn't

However, when authentic reconciliation does occur, our relationships can become more intimate and valuable than we have previously experienced. Enough to permit the final strategy.[8]

Strategy number two: We will seek to "carefront."

This term was coined by Augsberger to imply "speaking the truth in love." (See Ephesians 4:15.)

Carefronting means to courageously work through our own tensions and differences while lovingly seeking the other's optimum good. It is the perfect balance of confronting and caring.

Again, carefronting is only advisable when there is a measure of reconciliation through forgiveness. But once that occurs and carefronting begins to take place, the relationship is sure to deepen. And future episodes necessitating the need for additional forgiveness become increasingly less likely. Midcourse corrections are made before any major crisis occurs. And that's the way it should be.

Carefronting involves increased doses of both honesty and love. Carefronting means saying things such as, "I love you, brother, but you're starting to get on my

---

until age seventy-three that C. S. Lewis forgave his childhood schoolmaster. God forgives in a single swoosh. We can't always expect others to do so. "God forgives wholesale, we forgive retail." (c) Don't wait for the ideal time to forgive. Some say, I'll forgive after he thoroughly repents." That is unwise. Forgive, regardless of the offender's sorrow for past wrongs or his resolutions for future improvements. (d) Don't assume that forgiveness means a "Hollywood ending." We are not required to become close friends with those we forgive. Future relationships must take care of themselves.

Professor Smedes teaches ethics at Fuller Theological Seminary. Among the books he has written is *To Forgive and Forget: Healing the Hurt We Do Not Deserve* (San Francisco; Harper & Row, 1984).

8. David Augsberger, in his book *Caring Enough to Confront*, lays down seven "before" requirements for confronting. Prior to any confrontation (or carefrontation), these foundations must be established: A context of caring must exist before confrontation; a sense of support before criticism; an experience of empathy before evaluation; a basis of trust before one risks advising; a floor of affirmation before assertiveness; a gift of understanding before disagreeing. An awareness of love sets us free to level with each other. *The Christian Reader*, op. cit., p. 105.

nerves." "I know you don't mean to hurt me, but when you refer to my past, it's like a dagger into my heart." "Your continual neglect is beginning to be a real problem for me. Can we talk and pray together?"

Augsberger stated a truth when he said "[We] grow most rapidly when supported with the arm of loving respect, than confronted with the arm of clear honesty." In other words, when we practice carefronting.[9]

From Tears to Triumph

Earlier, I referred to my visit to Caesarea. That occurred on an anthropological study trip to the Middle East and Europe. Our stated purpose was to investigate archeological sites and study existing cultures. But my unstated goal was for us to receive inspiration. We weren't disappointed in either case.

One student traveler was the daughter of a well-known television actor. In her pretrip interview, she unashamedly expressed her love for Jesus and an overwhelming desire to visit the land where he had walked. For her it would be a pilgrimage.

On the trip we seemed to enter the pages of the Bible, recounting the moving stories and allowing the Savior to speak to our hearts.

A highlight was our visit to the traditional site where Jesus delivered his Sermon on the Mount. As we sat on large rocks, gazed out on the glistening Sea of Galilee, and read the moving sermon, all of us were greatly inspired.

Shortly thereafter, the young coed felt impressed to tell me how she found the Lord. Her story vividly illustrates how Jesus can help us to transcend the most difficult situations involving defiant people.

After two decades of marriage, her famous father de-

9. David Augsberger, "Caring Enough to Confront," in *How to Live the Holy Life: A Down-to-Earth Look at Holiness*, ed. Stephen M. Miller, pp. 67–75.

cided to leave her mother. The children were crushed. Her mother was demolished; bitterness rushed into her being, and she became completely miserable.

This bitterness was accentuated further when the celebrity married a much younger woman, someone whose age approximated that of his own daughter. The heart of my student's mother cried out, "How could he?"

Then something wonderful occurred. Her mother accepted Christ. Instantly, everything changed for this afflicted and tormented lady.

Through him she was able to completely forgive. And when she did, all traces of resentment instantly evaporated. The joy she felt exceeded all happiness she had ever experienced. She became, quite literally, a new person.

And so, near Galilee's shores that day, this student traveler looked at me and said, "Dr. Jon, I'll bet you're wondering why I became a Christian." I replied that I would be interested to know.

She continued, "It wasn't through hearing an inspirational sermon. Nor was it because I was raised in a Christian home." Then, with a face that exuded gratitude, she declared, "It was because of what Jesus did for my mom. He picked her up off the floor and completely transformed her life!"

When defiant, irregular persons hurt us grievously, we need not throw in the towel. It's not over until it's over. The one who picked up the towel to wipe his disciples' feet can turn our horror into hope. Our torture into triumph!

Footbridges must extend to the devoted—our friends. Drawbridges must reach to the defiant—our foes.

But can there be linkages between ourselves and those who are truly different? Persons from whom we're isolated? The next chapter attempts to answer these questions.

Prejudice is the child of ignorance.—Hazlitt

Cynics build no bridges; they make no discoveries; no gaps are spanned by them . . . the onward march of Christian civilization demands an inspiration and motivation that cynicism never affords.—Paul L. McKay

Many in today's church are content to be keepers of the aquarium rather than fishers of men.

7

Causeways to the Different

Animals behave in the strangest ways!

A lioness will not hesitate to consume her own cubs if alternative food sources are not available.

Stick a knife into a horse's side, but don't expect him to make a sound. Unlike the coyote, wolf, or other predator, he does not register pain in that manner.

And how about the unique ways that male animals flirt? The bowerbird strives to build a more beautiful love nest than his competitors. The desert iguana (lizard) performs rapid, attention-getting pushups. And the stickleback fish displays his bright red chest.

Animals seem so different from us. That's why we're intrigued by their behavior.

But, we are different from one another. We Americans are repulsed by even the thought of eating horse flesh, while persons from India react similarly toward the consumption of cattle. Germans refrain from drinking water, eating corn ("the food of swine"), and taking frequent baths. But, they won't hesitate to take their dogs into restaurants. We're the opposite on all counts.

As an anthropologist, I enjoy comparing cultural differences—and watching greenhorn tourists attempting to negotiate those differences. Take away pure tap water, washcloths, and toilet paper, and most American first-time travelers become extremely patriotic.

It's confession time. I must admit that I have real difficulty with international cuisine. My palate has remained embarrassingly selective. No sparrow on a stick, rat jerky, or worm burgers for me!

Case in point. On our last trip to the People's Republic of China, one of my Asian students intimidated me into eating a sea cucumber. I assumed that it must be a vegetable harvested from the ocean floor. After consuming the slithery object, Tian informed me that I had just eaten an oversized sea snail!

But, in spite of this and other equally repulsive culinary experiences, intercultural exposure has greatly enriched my life. Here are a couple reasons why.

First, it has expanded my perspective. To paraphrase anthropologist Peter Hammond, I've become increasingly "liberated from the prison of the tribal (my own people) and the intellectual tyranny of the contemporary (my own times)."[1]

I've emerged from my smug, cultural cocoon to experience God's great world.

Diverse cultures now seem like beautiful, multicolored Persian carpets. Unique. Creative. Exciting.

Second, my intercultural exposure has helped me to see myself more clearly.

---

1. Peter B. Hammond, *An Introduction to Cultural and Social Anthropology* (London: Macmillan Company, 1971).

Another pertinent comment by this author is, "Whatever is learned about men anywhere is ultimately relevant to understanding men everywhere" (p.25).

Different people have become mirrors that reflect who I really am.[2]

Strangers can be painfully candid. Why? Because they don't feel tied or obligated to us. When we lapse into ugly American behavior, they're likely to tell us so.

For these and many other reasons, we're encouraged to learn about others. By watching travelogues, reading anthropology books, and interacting with different persons, we can grow.

But, there is another side to this coin. Heightened awareness of cultural differences can also result in wall building. Differences are often perceived as threats. Consider what is happening in Northern Ireland, South Africa, and the Middle East.

Somehow, perceptions of our uniqueness become tangled with a powerful propensity toward prejudice. Let's see how.

Weighing Facts with Thumbs on the Scales

Theologian Martin Marty speaks of the "bigotry-brotherhood paradox." Its meaning is simple. The more intense our in-group morale, the thicker our walls. In other words, the more we like *us*, the more we detest *them*.

With this in mind, we clearly see that prejudice is like Topsy—it just grows. It is mostly unplanned, unexpected, and even unwanted. But, it doesn't hesitate to crash the party. And it usually does so in three stages:

2. Charles Horton Cooley, sociologist, coined the expression "looking-glass self." He compared other people to a mirror. We gaze into it, note how others respond to us, and as a result of their reactions we develop feelings about ourselves. That is, we gain a conception of self by reflection. The individual becomes largely what he understands his friends, acquaintances, and others with whom he interacts think he is. See Charles Horton Cooley, *Human Nature and the Social Order*, rev. ed., (New York: Schocken, 1964), chapters 5 and 6.

Stage 1   stereotyping (making a mental judgment that the different one is inferior);

Stage 2   prejudice (rejecting the different one emotionally and attitudinally;) and

Stage 3   discrimination (taking action to lash out at the different one)

Prejudice thrives in all cultures. Satan sees to that. Glynn Ross uses humor to describe prejudice. Note the underlying stereotypes.

> In heaven
>   the chefs are French,
>   the police are English,
>   the lovers are Italian,
>   the mechanics are German,
>   and the whole place is run by the Swiss.
> In hell
>   the chefs are English,
>   the police are German,
>   the lovers are Swiss,
>   the mechanics are French,
>   and the whole place is run by the Italians.[3]

Prejudice is reflected in literature. Consider these proverbs:

Italian: "The Italian is wise when he undertakes a thing; the German while he is doing it; and a Frenchman when it is over."

Arabian: "The difference between Arabs and Persians is the same as that between a date and stone."

When cultures are so prejudicial that they become obsessed with their own uniqueness, they are said to be ethnocentric. In short, they see themselves as the measur-

---

3. *New Times*, May 28–June 3, 1986, Glynn Ross (Artistic Director, Arizona Opera Company).

ing stick for everyone else.[4] To the degree that the others differ, they are considered to be inferior.

On the South Sea island Bali, the natives look upon American tourists with pity. Their reasoning goes something like this. We Balinese never leave our country because we love it so much. But those Americans, who wear funny looking polka dot shorts and carry big cameras, show a lot of interest in our ways. That must mean that they despise their homeland and wish that they could be us.

But that's Bali. Does ethnocentrism exist inside our churches? Yes. In fact, it flourishes.

A Divine Blunder?

Who are the widespread targets of abuse among Christians?

While eating lunch recently, someone said, "Something really concerns me. Why would a good God create

---

4. According to Eskimo beliefs, the first man, though made by the Great Being, was a failure, and was consequently cast aside and called *kob-lu-na*, which means "white man." But a second attempt of the Great Being resulted in the formation of a perfect man, and he was called *In-nu*, the name the Eskimo gave to themselves.

When anything foolish is done, the Chippewas use an expression which means "as stupid as a white man."

The Veddah of Ceylon have a very high opinion of themselves and regard their civilized neighbors with contempt.

When Greenlanders see a foreigner of gentle and modest manners, their usual remark is, "He is almost as well-bred as we."

Most preliterates regard their own people as "the" people, as the root of all others, and as occupying the middle of the earth. The Hottentots love to call themselves "the men of men." The Aborigines of Haiti believed that their island was the first of all things, that the sun and moon issued from one of its caverns, and men from another.

The Chinese were taught to think of themselves as being superior to all peoples. According to Japanese ideas, Nippon was the first country created and the center of the world.

The Greeks called Delphi, or rather the round stone in the Delphic temples the "navel" or the "middle point of the earth." Howard Becker and Harry Elmer Barnes, *Social Thought From Lore to Science*, Third edition, Vol. 1 (New York: Dover Publications, Incorporated, 1961), Chapter 1, pp. 3–42.

so many different kinds of people, knowing full well that our differences cause us to dislike one another?"

My immediate response was, "No way! I'm not about to allow my heavenly Father to receive the rap for our prejudice."

He created a rich variety of cultures to add beauty to his planet. His plan is for us to perceive that his creation is good, just as he confirmed that it was (Gen. 1:31).

He desires that we openly and lovingly accept all that he has created. His matchless handiwork in nature. But even more, all humanity, which is the apex of his creation.

Prejudice is Satan's invention. God's people must reject it. Emphatically. Finally.

Deep down, those of us who have accepted God's Son as our Savior understand this truth, for it is so basically biblical.

However, many of us are far from being purged of a prejudicial spirit. Even though we attend church. In a sense, we're like some of our forefathers, who "went to God's House to pray on their *knees*—but on their way home, they preyed on the *Aborigines* (Indians)!"

We sing "Holy, Holy, Holy, Lord God Almighty." At the same time, we harbor ill feelings toward those whom through his might he has created.

We send vast sums to missionaries in Africa, while neglecting to realize that there is an "Africa" on this side of the Atlantic.

When it comes to whom of our members we transgress, we're up front and consistent; We can easily pinpoint the lepers in our midst. In our minds, their spots betray them.

Lyle E. Schaller provides this list of popular undesirables. When we dispense our prejudice, they are the targets likely to receive a generous supply.

Our Targets

ethnics (especially blacks, Indians, Mexicans, Puerto Ricans, Koreans, Filipinos)	mentally retarded or ill	persons in wheelchairs
people uncomfortable with our style of worship or theology	widows	childless couples
teenagers	single parents	divorced and remarried
illiterates	single adults (especially males)	unmarried couples living together
the very poor	alcoholics	non-Christians
drug addicts	the extremely shy	people who dress poorly
deaf or hard-of-hearing	people who work on Sundays	radical dissenters (or extremely creative)
	couples and children of interracial marriages	lacking verbal skills
	visually handicapped	physically deformed[5]

To this list can be added the homeless, aged, orphans, victims of disease (e.g., AIDS), homosexuals, obese. All have one thing in common. They are different enough from the majority, who consider them to be lowly. They are the kind of people to whom Jesus offered kind and special attention.

But the question is, why do we shun the very sheep that our Lord reached out to? Let's explore two possible reasons.

First, often we fear unfamiliar persons. And our fear translates into a crippling shyness.

During the last decade, psychologist Philip Zimbardo and his Stanford University colleagues examined shyness, which they term the prisoner within.

They explain that shy persons receive continuous "in-

5. Lyle E. Schaller, *Assimilating New Members* (Nashville: Abingdon Press, 1978), pp. 49–50. This list is slightly modified.

ner commands from the guard self"—commands that activate inhibitions. The guard self says things such as, "If you do that (raise your hand, sing, be friendly), you'll look ridiculous. The only way to be safe is to be unseen and unheard."[6]

Result: the prisoner within meekly complies and withdraws. Hawthorne probably had shyness in mind when he penned these words:

> What other dungeon is so dark
> —as one's heart?
> What jailer so inexorable
> —as one's self?[7]

Shyness exists in epidemic proportions, and can rightfully be considered a social disease. Zimbardo found that 80 percent admit to having been shy at some point in their lives, and of these 40 percent see themselves as presently shy. Twenty-five percent disclose that for them shyness is a chronic condition.

Perhaps the best term to describe the effects of shyness is "reticence." It means an exaggerated reluctance to relate to others, especially strangers.

When forced to interact, the reticent person typically has butterflies within and blushing without. These reactions are often accompanied by painful self-consciousness, guilt, and loneliness. (If you are afflicted with shyness or are curious about it, please take the Stanford Shyness Survey in Appendix 1.)

Many of us resemble the rabbit-hole Christians whom theologian John Stott describes. Only when it's absolutely necessary do we shyly pop out of our holes, scurry to people unlike ourselves, then quickly rush back into

---

6. Quoted by Philip G. Zimbardo, *Shyness: What It Is, What To do About It* (New York: Jove Publications, 1977), pp. 25, 39.

7. Ibid., p. 16.

our holes again. To linger outside, we reason, is to risk great danger. We're afraid of our shadows.

Second, in addition to being fearful, we forget about the people outside our circles of security who need us. We're so caught up with our safe and familiar cronies that we wall out the others. Friends so dominate our time and energy that meaningful involvement with others is precluded.

It's so ironic. Those of us who forget about others are usually unaware of our omissions. We're basically decent people. It's not our design to hurt anyone by either intent or neglect.

But make no mistake about it, we often seem cruel to those we forget. They feel the full impact of our slights. They're emotionally broadsided when we do such things as turn our backs, refuse to have eye contact, or communicate some other you-don't-count message.

As followers of Jesus, we're to neither fear nor forget persons who differ from ourselves. Like Jesus, we must devote an inordinate amount of attention to such persons. If we in the church don't, who will?

But this requires concentration and sacrificial effort. The kind that Jesus describes in his Parable of the Good Samaritan.

Where's the "Triple A" When You Need Them?

In a very real sense, we are all expected to be Good Samaritans, and that means becoming truly neighborly to those who are not our own kind.

Let's recall Jesus' story by focusing on its principal characters.

First, there was the traveler who was obviously reckless and foolhardy. He embarked on the notoriously dangerous road from Jerusalem to Jericho.[8] Over its twenty-mile span, it drops 3,600 feet in altitude. Besides being extremely narrow and winding, it was the happy hunting ground of robbers. Nobody in their right mind would have set out on it alone. Nevertheless, this Jewish traveler did, and he was waylaid.

Enter character number two, the priest. After a quick glance at the poor man's plight, he turned into a road-runner. While streaking by, he likely remembered that anyone who touched a dead man was considered unclean for seven days (Num. 19:11). Why take the chance?

If he stopped, touched, and found the man to be dead, he must lose his turn of duty in the Temple.

Here was a man who cared more for ceremony than charity. More for liturgy than providing a loving lift!

Third, there was the Levite. The chances are that he realized that bandits often used decoys. One would act wounded; then when a good-hearted person stopped to help, the other robbers would pounce on him. Reassuring himself that his mother hadn't raised a fool, the Levite felt justified in passing by. For him, it was safety first.

Finally, down the road came the Samaritan. A hated half breed from the region of that name—a region that orthodox Jews avoided.[9]

Two important features set him apart from the other

8. William Barclay furnishes useful background on the treachery of this infamous road which still exists. It now winds around the modern highway that was constructed this century, and is hiked upon by many.

"In the fifth century Jerome tells us that it was still called 'The Red, or Bloody Way.' In the nineteenth century it was still necessary to pay safety money to the local sheiks before one could travel on it. As late as the early 1930s, H. V. Morton tells us that he was warned to get home before dark if he intended to use the road, because a certain Abu Jildah was an adept [criminal] at holding up cars and robbing travelers and tourists, and escaping to the hills before the police could arrive. When Jesus told this story, he was telling about the kind of thing that was constantly happening on this Jerusalem to Jericho road." William Barclay, *Daily Study Bible: The Gospel of Luke* (Philadelphia: The Westminster Press, 1953), p. 141.

9. Ibid., p. 143. According to Barclay, the Samaritan may have been a "racial Samaritan"—a hated half breed from the region of that name which orthodox Jews avoided. Or, he could have been someone considered ceremonially unclean. The Jews called such persons by that name. Even Jesus was so tagged. (John 8:48)

passersby. For one thing, only he was determined to assist. Notice the Luke 10:33–35 progression. He "came where the man was" (proximity), "took pity" (compassion), "bandaged his wounds, pouring on oil and wine" (crisis intervention), "took him to an inn" (donkey ambulance service), "took care of him" (nursing), gave "two silver coins . . . to the innkeeper" (financing short-term care), and said, "'When I return, I will reimburse you for any extra expense'" (financing long-term care).

A second noteworthy fact about the Samaritan was that his credit was good. The innkeeper placed implicit trust in his promise to pay later. He was recognized as an honest person in a day of rampant dishonesty.

Nice story. Great ending, the kind that Hollywood likes. A tale that we can hear and forget? Not quite. Scottish theologian William Barclay admonishes us to derive from it these valuable lessons:

1. People must be helped, even when they bring trouble on themselves—as the traveler did.

2. Regardless of how different from ourselves they are, people who are in need must be thought of as our closest neighbors.

3. Compassion in theory is not compassion at all. We must dispense tangible help.

After fully digesting these truths, we must vow to model our lives after the Good Samaritan. His approach to persons different from himself must become our approach. How do we know? Because our Lord said so. After concluding the parable, his words to his audience were (and are), "Go and do likewise." (v. 37)[10]

---

10. The Samaritan stopped, stooped, and stayed. Then he carried, cared for, and became committed to (leaving an open bill).

Another perspective is offered by theologian and author Ralph Earle. He contrasts the principal characters this way: *robbers*: Their approach is beat him up, and their attitude is, "What belongs to you is mine—I'll take it." *priest and Levite*: Their approach is pass him

Are there any tips for fulfilling this important mission? I think so. Allow me to suggest a few.

The World's Longest Rafts

During our last trip to Florida, some friends suggested that we all travel down to the Keys to get some key lime pie. Believe me, the pie was well worth the trip. So was the beautiful scenery. Swooping seagulls. Clear skies. Whitecaps.

Actually, the Keys resemble a string of pearls going southward off the Florida coast. They are connected by bridges called causeways. Now, these bridges are unique, for they actually float on the surface of the water. This gives them flexibility when hammered by the frequent tropical storms.

If linkages with friends are like footbridges, and linkages with foes resemble drawbridges, the bridges we build toward the persons different from us are like causeways. They are flexible, adaptive, and extend great distances.

In constructing such expansive structures toward outsiders, here are some of the things we keep in mind.

Discipling the Different

To begin, when reaching out causeway style to persons who are distinctively different from ourselves, it is important that we cease thinking hierarchically. We must reject our natural inclination to measure people and to respond to them according to our assessment of their importance.

It's time to realize that cultivating oneness necessitates our becoming unimpressed by titles, authority ladders,

---

up, and their attitude is, "What belongs to me is mine—I'll keep it." *Samaritan*: His approach is help him up, and his attitude is, "What belongs to me is yours—I'll give it."

From a lecture at Nazarene Theological Seminary, 1966.

status symbols, and awards. Listen to James' pronouncement.

> My brothers, as believers in our glorious Lord Jesus Christ, don't show favoritism. Suppose a man comes into your meeting wearing a gold ring and fine clothes, and a poor man in shabby clothes. . . . If you show special attention to the man wearing fine clothes and say, "Here's a good seat for you," but say to the poor man, "You stand there," . . . have you not discriminated among yourselves? . . . If you show favoritism, you sin. . . James 2:1–4, 9).

If we would only grasp how much our Lord despises all semblances of elitism and its grotesque first cousins cronyism and nepotism! To him, it matters not

how much money a person makes (i.e., giving potential);

how famous he is in the world or church;

who he is related to, that is (or once was) renowned; nor

how long he has been a Christian

Someone said it well "At the foot of the cross, all ground is level." To Christ we are all on equal footing. Therefore, when reaching out to different people, we must admonish ourselves to not be respecters of persons. Regardless of how much our church needs money, or regardless of our craving for friends with clout.

Another suggestion. In attempting to relate to different people, we must go beyond trying to be nice. Outsiders are turned off by our saccharine smiles, backslaps, and glad-handing. They don't want to be processed as persons are at used-car lots and political rallies.

As Moishe Rosen states, "The early Christians didn't

post a slogan on a church announcement board stating, 'Come to the friendliest place in town.'"[11]

The same author assures us that God never commanded his people to be nice and congenial. He requires them to love one another, which involves "proper attitudes and unselfish acts that promote [their] best interests."[12]

Niceness isn't enough. We're to be far more than experts in public relations. Courtesy and good manners are basic requirements, but we must go beyond that. Otherwise, we're likely to only win people to ourselves and not to Jesus Christ.

Acceptance of people is more than a posture, it's a position. It's more than a smile and "an affable greeting or exchange of pleasantries." It is a commitment to be someone—something—to those who feel different and estranged. True acceptance transcends being nice to persons in an occasional social encounter; rather, it implies standing with them in the midst of their unpleasantness.

I don't know about you, but when I feel excluded, I prefer someone dour who relates to me authentically over a person who smiles and relates superficially.

My appeal is simple. We must stop trying to be merely nice, merely friendly. All such self-engineered attempts can only produce a veneer of acceptance.

Instead of *trying* to be nice, we must *be* nice—from our hearts outward. Our loving acceptance of different persons must come from the overflow of Christ's presence inside us.

Finally, when the different ones are enslaved by sin, we must help them to accept Jesus into their lives. Our primary purpose on earth, as Christians, is to make disciples for the master (see Acts 1:8). Our unprejudiced and

---

11. Moishe Rosen, "Don't Try to Be Nice," *The Jews for Jesus Newsletter*, Vol. 10:5745
12. Ibid.

complete acceptance of them is not enough. Our relationship must draw others to him.

Are there practical strategies for leading such people to the Lord? Yes. They are offered by Win and Charles Arn in their book *The Master's Plan for Making Disciples*. Here is a summary of their useful suggestions.

1. Cease being timid. Boldly venture out from behind the wall of fear and risk failure for Jesus.

2. Make God's top priority—soul winning—your own. Make this your favorite hobby, and give it generous amounts of time and energy.

3. Become increasingly reliant on and sensitive to the Holy Spirit. As your comforter and guide, he will use your words to convict others of sin.

4. Know your Bible. To spread the Word, you must thoroughly grasp what it says and means.

5. Join with others who share your burden for the lost. A support group provides needed accountability, courage, faith, and honest feedback.

6. Learn the dynamics of effectively relating in all environments to all kinds of people. No matter what your temperament is, grasp principles that will allow you and God to penetrate walls of resistance.

7. Expand your sphere of influence. Go beyond family, neighbors, and friends—though the latter must not be neglected.

8. Meet more than spiritual needs. Every non-Christian has a "handle of interest" and a "handle of need." By relating to the former, or giving support to the latter, people become more open to the good news of salvation.[13]

13. Win Arn and Charles Arn, *The Master's Plan for Making Disciples* (Kansas City, MO: Beacon Hill Press, 1982), pp. 14–30.

Forget thinking in terms of hierarchies. Accept all persons on equal footing. They have nothing to prove to Jesus, why should they to us? So, go far beyond superficial niceness. Express a congeniality that overflows from a pure, Spirit-filled heart.

But, most important, we must allow Jesus to help us to lead those who are outside of the ark of salvation to a saving assurance of sins forgiven. He can make every one of us soul winners. And he can begin to do it immediately.

It's Up and Over!

Father Damian. Does the name mean anything to you? It didn't to me until I heard his gripping story.

Many years ago, leprosy was common in the Hawaiian Islands. Victims of this dreaded, deadly contagious disease were quarantined on Hawaii's island Molokai. Isolated. Alone to suffer. Without hope.

Then, our faithful Savior tapped a lowly Catholic priest, Father Damian, to minister to his leprous sheep. Father Damian obeyed.

From outside the walls of their encampment, the loving minister called out words of encouragement and hope. The people listened intently, but they remained quite detached. Words are cheap when they come from non-sufferer to sufferer. And Father Damian, as none other, realized this fact.

His burden weighed more heavily each day. He prayed that he might somehow get through to these estranged people. Then, our Lord heard and provided him with an answer. An answer that he least expected but willingly accepted.

One Sunday morning the good priest addressed his suffering congregation. But this time it was different. No longer did a wall separate him from the lepers, for he had entered their compound.

His captivating words rang out that day. Words that have been etched on my mind since I first heard them

"My friends, before, I have always begun my sermon by addressing you as *you* lepers. This morning I say *we* lepers."

Father Damian paid the ultimate sacrifice to reach Molokai's perishing lepers. He intimately identified with their plight. As we might expect, the sufferers were profoundly moved by this identification. And they began to dramatically respond to the good news that he preached. A genuine spiritual renewal took place in that compound.

It all happened because a dedicated priest built a causeway of love to some desperate, different people. Even though eventually it cost him his life.

As with the devoted and the defiant, we must lovingly link ourselves with the different.

Challenging? Absolutely. But, with God's power fueling our energies and inspiring our hearts, we can meet the challenge.

There is still one last kind of bridge we must construct. This one is to the distant or indifferent.

For many of us, this is the most difficult of all to build. It will require our best endeavors, together with the best that God can give us.

The seven last words of the church are, "We never did it that way before."

The grave itself is but a covered bridge
Leading from light to light, through a brief darkness.
            —Henry Wadsworth Longfellow "A Covered
                Bridge at Lucern"

At age twenty we worry about what others think of us; at
forty we don't care what others think of us; at sixty we
discover that others haven't been thinking of us at all!

8

Covered Bridges to the Distant

This tongue-in-cheek notice may not strike all of us as humorous. Only those of us who have been employed at such places as I have.

Notice to All Employees

It has come to the attention of the management that employees have been dying on the job and either refusing or neglecting to keel over. This practice must stop. Any employee found dead on the job, either in an upright or prone position, will immediately be dropped from the payroll.

In the future, if a supervisor notices that any employee has made no movement for a period of two hours, it will be his duty to investigate. As it is almost impossible to distinguish between death and the natural movement of some employees, supervisors are cautioned to make a careful investigation.

Holding a paycheck in front of the suspected employee is generally considered an authentic test,
but there have been cases reported where the natural instinct has been so deeply embedded that the
hand of the employee has made a spasmodic clutch
even after rigor mortis has set in.

The Management.[1]

We have all sorts of names for this malady: apathy,
listlessness, halfheartedness, detachment, turned off.

When the malady is job-related, our work becomes
sheer duty. Someone defined "duty" as "what we look
forward to with distaste, do with reluctance, and boast
about forever after." Duty implies boredom. A grind. A
slow burn. An absence of enthusiasm.

When the same spirit of detachment characterizes relationships with other persons, it is even more tragic. We
then feel alienated. Alone. Distant. And this feeling can
be even more prevalent when we're in a crowd. Every
person who pushes or bumps into us only reinforces our
dispirited attitudes.

Distancing ourselves from others can occur in two
ways. First, we can push off and become isolated. This
implies physically separating ourselves from others. We,
quite literally, become "islands" surrounded by tall, thick
walls.

Such is the plight of American Indians who reside on
reservations. When first placed there, they made awkward attempts to escape and recapture what they had lost,
only to face impenetrable walls of rejection.

Now, scores of them have rediscovered the value of
their uniqueness. An about-face has occurred. They've
built some formidable walls of their own. Recently, one
chief vividly expressed this strong sentiment: "White

---

1. Seen on a plaque produced by Ogunquit Corporation, Costa Mesa, California.

man, the fences that you built to *keep us in* are now intended to *keep you out!*"[2] (ital. mine)

A second way that we unplug ourselves from the electrical current of social involvement is by becoming insulated. By becoming immune and oblivious. Numbed and desensitized.

This usually occurs gradually. We scarcely recognize that we're pulling away, for we may very well remain physically close.

A classic experiment in biology class comes to mind. The professor places a twisting, wiggling frog into a glass container filled with water. The amphibious creature glides through the water with ease and obvious delight.

Then, a Bunsen burner is placed under the small tank. The fire is lit, but only the smallest possible flame is exposed. The cold water ever-so-gradually gets warmer. But our little green friend never notices that this is taking place.

A few hours later the experiment is all over. The frog has been cooked. No struggle. No splashing. No attempts to escape.

When we gradually insulate ourselves from others we, likewise, can become desensitized. We're decreasingly aware of the slow death that is beginning to paralyze our relationships.

Wives, children, and church friends may become alarmed and warn us.

We assure them that we haven't noticed anything, saying, "Relax. Don't worry. Things are fine." Meanwhile, our circulation continues to ebb as we cook.

2. The term revitalization, coined by A. F. C. Wallace, is frequently applied to such radical responses. Such brash reactions are a means of coping with tension experienced by members of simple, small-scale cultures when contacts with technologically more advanced ones threaten their traditional way of life. It's a way of saying, "We have value." Such responses or movements, which are intended to achieve an ideologically effective response to rapidly shifting or discouraging circumstances, are also described as "nativistic," "messianic," or "millenarian." Examples are the ghost dance of the Plains Indians; Cargo Cults of the South Pacific.

See Peter B. Hammond, *An Introduction to Cultural and Social Anthropology* (New York: Macmillan Company, 1971), p. 272.

The point is clear: Isolation and insulation are real killers.

Therefore we Christian bridge builders first of all must consciously avoid cutting ourselves off from others. God made us all to be social persons—regardless of our temperaments or natural inclinations. Without meaningful relationships, everyone's psyches would shrivel.

Second, with desire and skill we must build bridges to persons who have pushed away from us. And we must do it even if they resist.

It is important to remember that distant persons are usually unaware of their pitiful and terminal conditions. Like the frog, they're becoming desensitized by degrees. Thus, even if they rebuff us, we must continue to reach out to them in love. Edwin Markham captures this perspective in his poem entitled "Outwitted."

> He drew a circle that shut me out—
> Heretic, rebel, a thing to flout;
> But Love and I had the wit to win:
> We drew a circle that took him in![3]

Bridge Beauty-Contest Winner

As you've probably guessed, the imagery of another bridge invades my consciousness. Allow me to share it.

Line them up. All the bridges we've described, plus any others we can think of. In my view, none is more picturesque or romantic than the classic covered bridge. But don't take only my word for it. Ask anyone in New England, where such structures dot the landscape.

Ask the air force pilots who flew in World War II. In addition to locating and bombing the elusive enemy, they were commanded to avoid dropping explosives on the centuries-old covered bridges of Europe.

3. *An Anthology of American Poetry*, ed. Alfred Kreymborg (New York: Tudor Publishing Company, 1930), p. 214.

Case in point. The famous Ponte Vecchio Bridge of Florence, Italy, majestically spans the Arno River. It is lined with quaint, old-world shops—and is a camera buff's delight. All other bridges in the area were hit, but this piece of history was declared off limits. In the midst of the fire and rubble, it remained completely unscathed.[4]

Then there is my favorite covered bridge. It is the rustic Chapel Bridge, located in Lucerne, Switzerland. Constructed in 1333 over the Reuss River, it was meant to fortify the city. Gables overhead feature paintings by the seventeenth-century artist Heinrich Wagmann depicting the city's history. A multitude of swans glide through the waters below.[5]

We say to ourselves, "Granted, covered bridges are beautiful. But what is their connection with the kind of relationships that link us with people who are distant?"

Well, to most of us, covered bridges suggest a feeling of warmth and friendliness. When we enter them, in our cars or on foot, we seem to be drawn together in a snug environment of intimacy. The darkness and close quarters seem to enwrap us together in a place of concealment and protection. Covered bridges are like proverbial tunnels of love.[6]

4. The Ponte Vecchio's history extends back to the era that preceded Christ's birth. When Emperor Hadrian repaired the Via Cassia (Road to Rome) in A.D. 1200, the bridge was given a masonry and wood edifice. From that time on, it witnessed the steps of legionnaires and the roll of farmers' and merchants' carts as they brought goods to the city.

In 1333 there was a great flood that destroyed the bridge. It was again intact by 1345. In its rebuilt state, it was conceived as a street with two rows of houses along its sides. (This was never thought of before nor seen afterwards.) Then, the bridge turned into a meat market during the sixteenth century. The shopkeepers built rooms that extended over the river. Finally, the goldsmiths moved in offering some of the finest jewelry in the world. Today it still has shops on both sides of a walkway.

The world-famous structure was studiously avoided during the bombing raids of the Allied Forces in World War II. Piero Bargellini, *This is Florence* (Florence: G. C. Sansoni Editore Nuovo S. P. A., 1977).

5. At the bridge's midpoint is a stone, octagonal-shaped water tower. This has served as a defense post, dungeon, and a place to store archives throughout the centuries.

6. But not all covered bridges connote such positive feelings. North of Rome is Venice, the "City of Canals" and home of the famous covered Bridge of Sighs. It is an ornate, concrete transept that connects two ancient buildings, Doge's Palace and the State Prison. Built by Antoni Contoni in the 1500s and described in Lord Byron's "Childe Harold's

In reaching out to isolated and insulated persons, these are the very feelings that we must communicate so that they sense our warmth, closeness, and desire for intimacy. From us they must pick up definite cues that we consider them to be very special.

Furthermore, in communicating this private "care bear" message, we must in a very real sense shut out the noise of the outside world. It must be just us and them. Alone. Together. Intimate.

Such intense feelings and focused attention can do wonders for even the most emotionally immobilized persons. Their numbness can begin to vanish, their spirits start to kindle. Just as they gradually became emotional zombies, they can gradually become real, live, pulsating persons again. In short, they can be liberated from the lonely prison walls that they have constructed.

But, before we attempt such noble and empathetic ventures, it is crucial that we understand how such persons became victims. Allow me to suggest some possible answers.

The Desensitizers

The kind of emotional numbness that overtakes those of us who become distant and indifferent usually begins with our perceived threat of pain.

We protect ourselves by withdrawing. It's the old if-you-can't-fight-it-flee-it syndrome. And our constricture leads to desensitization.

Pilgrimage," this structure contains two passages. Through one, the accused went to trial. Through the other, the condemned went to their execution.

How did the bridge get its unusual name? It is said that prisoners en route to their deaths would pause on it, have one last look at their beloved city, take a deep sigh, and then move on to the inevitable.

So venerated is this bridge that replicas of it exist at Cambridge University in England, as well as in New York City. In the latter location, it connects Tombs Prison and what was formerly the criminal courts. Prisoners once used this passageway "in order to avoid [the gazes and comments of] street pedestrians." See "Bridge of Sighs," *The World Book Encyclopedia*, Wm. Nault, ed. (Chicago: World Books, Inc., 1987).

Modern society pushes us to retreat. How? By overloading us with stressful experiences.

Many of us receive more stimulation than we can adequately process. Our minds and emotions can't keep up. We buzz-out. Social psychologists term this phenomenon "psychic overload."

Our constitutions can only take so much stress. Beyond that point, a deterioration of emotional and/or physical health is likely to occur.

Furthermore, our relationships are apt to suffer. This is why persons contracting debilitating illnesses often get divorces. Why parents who lose a child frequently turn on each other. Inordinate amounts of stress cause us to search for scapegoats.

T. H. Holmes and R. H. Rahe have rated stress events according to their impact on our well-being. Their assessment of the impact of the top ten (of forty-three) stressful life events looks like this:

Rank	Life Event	Life Change Unit Value (note: maximum stress = 100)
1	Death of a spouse	100
2	Divorce	73
3	Marital separation	65
4	Jail term	63
5	Death of a close family member	63
6	Personal injury or illness	53
7	Marriage	50
8	Fired from job	47
9	Marital reconciliation	45
10	Retirement	45[7]

7. Irving Wallace, *The Book of Lists #2* (New York: Bantam Books, 1980), pp. 362–363.

(For the complete list of forty-three "Life Events" see Appendix 2, and for lists of "Highest and Lowest Pressure Jobs in the U.S.A." see Appendix 3.)

Again, when our coping mechanism malfunctions because of such stress-related overload, we're likely to give up. At such times, the words of Jesus become the grand oasis in our bleak desert. "Come to me, all you who are weary and burdened, and I will give you rest" (Matt. 11:28).

In addition to overwhelming stress, we're desensitized by two activities that consume much of our time. What are they?

First, watching our televisions. The desensitizing effects of television overdose are undeniable.

Television has the advantage of being edited. Therefore, it is nearly flawless in its production. If we are not careful, its quality can prompt us to expect near perfection from persons we encounter.

Also, television can engender impatience. Its programming is rapid fire. Its delivery is immediate. We're conditioned to expect to be constantly entertained. Result: We begin to expect instant everything. The word *wait* is deleted from our vocabulary.

But, most important of all, television has had a hardening effect on our minds and emotions. We have come to fear little and grieve even less.

When movies were first made, some persons would faint at the sight of an oncoming train. By contrast, today's children clamor for monster-thrillers, and parents barely wince at the tragic events shown on the evening news.

Television desensitizes. Thus, it lessens our compassion and dulls our willingness to reach out in love.

Another modern desensitizing activity is driving our cars.

Jesus walked. Even at his steady gait he could only hope to travel thirty miles per day. By contrast, we blitz down the highway, unless we enter the halo zone of a police car.

When Jesus walked, people could and did have meaningful encounters with him. He was approachable.

People can't possibly approach us when we are strapped in our multihorsepowered chariots of fire. We rush by them—even those who are beside the road in distress—like the priest and Levite of old.

Here's something else. Our automobiles have allowed us to live in suburbia, away from the decadent inner city with its masses of undesirables. To us, those other persons don't really exist.

Stress overload. Television. Cars. They combine to numb us, so that we no longer truly feel for our distant fellow man.

We must break through these walls. There must be an encounter—so that our lives interface with the indifferent.

This must take place in the world, but even more so in our churches. There, it should be impossible for us to remain distant. Circles must be drawn "to take us in."

But who are we talking about? To which of us should our churches devote special, concentrated attention? Let's focus on two distant-prone groups. The first is insulated, and the second is isolated.

Singles: Going It Alone

One fifth of all families in America have single parents, and that's an 80 percent increase in the past ten years. One-half of all children born today can expect to live with only one parent.

Stereotypes of singles are that they typically manifest these undesirable characteristics: hostility toward marriage and the opposite sex, homosexual tendencies, unattractiveness, fixation on parents, physical disability, inability to attract a mate, extreme loneliness. The conclusion: To think that singlehood leads to happiness is to be deluded.[8]

Unfortunately, our churches have accepted this negative stereotype as much as anyone. While businesses see singles as goldmines, our religious enclaves picture them as pariahs or victimized unfortunates.[9] In addition, we Christians characteristically consider the nuclear family (dad, mom, and the children) as God-ordained and sacrosanct.

To compensate for this glaring and blatant intimidation of singles, some Christians have attempted to minister to them. Creative programs and sensitive materials have emerged. We should applaud and support such efforts.[10] Not only that, we must support them.

8. Considering their rapidly growing numbers, it is surprising that sociology and psychology has not produced a plethora of books on singles. Most likely, the reason is this: They are perceived as being in transition—on their way to being remarried or (if aged) deceased. As Carolyn Koons states, "Sociology and psychology must wake up and do serious research on the singles phenomenon, for it is here to stay!" See Robert White, *Going It Alone: The Family Life and Social Situations* (New York: Basic, 1981)

9. The world of business realizes that singles are responsible for its largest single pool of sales. In short, singles make or break products. For this reason, business does all it can to relate to this booming market. Commercials depict young, attractive, free-spirited, athletic persons. Appliances are geared to singles: single burners for weiners ("The Hot Dogger") and coffee ("Mr. Coffee"); one-person refrigerators, washers and dryers. Automobiles are made much smaller, with youthful styling. Footwear is made to appeal to the recreationally-minded singles. Real estate favors condo living, which is best suited for this affluent group. (Information extracted from a recent lecture by Carolyn Koons.)

10. Author Harold Ivan Smith leads an organization called Tear Catchers, which ministers to persons who have experienced divorce. Multitudes of similar programs exist, especially in large churches, for those who never married, who possess homosexual tendencies, whose spouses are deceased, etc.

Most of these programs, like Tear Catchers, are commendable. But I have some real problems with others. First, some cultivate a hedonistic world view. Enjoyment is their only purpose. There is more to Christian singledom than ski trips and swimming parties. Singles must have fun, but more important, they must become involved in helping-hand ministries. They must become givers far more than takers.

Secondly, singles' programs often over emphasize the value of being single. This is unfortunate. Granted, singles must rid themselves of inferiority complexes, but *not* by becoming egotistical. Elton Trueblood spoke the truth when he once said to me, "There is a real danger in giving undue emphasis to our own uniqueness."

Finally, some programs engender isolation and insulation from the church body. Separateness breeds loneliness, defeating idiosyncrasies, and inability to relate in an effective manner. Christian singles must refuse to become "groupies." To do so is to be considered odd by others, who draw conclusions with the only information accessible to them.

Singles specialist Carolyn Koons offers people in local churches ten outstanding suggestions for ministering to these persons whose natural inclination is to become distant and uninvolved.

1. No more band-aid ministry to singles. They are broken, and we must freely and generously offer hope.

2. This isn't just another specialized ministry like caring for the handicapped. Singles must be perceived as and incorporated into the church body.

3. We must redefine our concept of family. In addition to nuclear, there are extended, expanded, blended, single, etc. We must accept all types equally.

4. Barriers that separate marrieds from singles must be smashed. Don't separate them physically or programmatically.

5. Forget about overseeing singles. There's no need for insulting chaperones, or a chaperone mentality.

6. Encourage singles to become leaders in our churches. This sends the right signals to the congregation, and affirms other singles.

7. Let's make our churches places of refuge for singles. For their tough times, we must offer them a loving support group.

8. Emphasize the New Testament concept of community. Play down differences and uniqueness—accentuate our oneness in Christ.

9. We must become equippers rather than directors. Singles chafe under the direction of benevolent dic-

---

It is imperative that singles work into the mainstream of the church. This implies involvement with everyone. Forget about homogeneous enclaves, regardless of what church growth theorists say. The New Testament model is one of heterogeneity, different kinds of people forming a loving community, where authentic fellowship exists, all because they have the most binding thing in common—their oneness in Christ!

tators. They need to be taught to minister to one another as leaders (responsible for themselves) and healers (ministering to mutual hurts).

10. Most important, our singles programs must have spiritual power and depth. To go on a binge of fun-type activities is to encourage shallowness. Prayer retreats and compassionate projects, by contrast, build spiritual muscle.[11]

It's tough to go it alone. No singles in our churches should have to do so if the rest of us are being the kind of disciples that Jesus expects us to be.

There is a second distant group which is likewise commonly overlooked. Unlike the first, however, they have physically removed themselves from the church premises. They've checked out completely. And often for understandable reasons.

Dropouts: When Love Webs Tear Apart

The Narrows Bridge in Tacoma, Washington, looked as sturdy as any in the country. Its handsome beams glistened in the sunshine. Its strong cables were the picture of security.

But one day something amazing occurred. A powerful crosswind did a number on this structure. It swayed left and right, then suddenly, another crosswind gave it a terrific up and down movement. In a matter of seconds it completely disintegrated—before the lens of a tourist's movie camera.[12]

This scene reminds me of another bridge falling that is equally tragic, namely, the disintegration of relationships between persons and their churches.

11. Taken from the previously referred-to lecture by Carolyn Koons.
12. The often-shown movie of this spectacular collapse, taken by a tourist, reveals what occurred that day. A single automobile started to cross. The rumble began. The man immediately stopped his car, grabbed his dog, and began running to safety. He barely made it before the collapse.

Such persons, whom I term dropouts, are found all over. I've spoken with more than a few. Many delight in describing former days of close communion. But their eyes become downcast as they cite circumstances that led to the dissolution of that communion. They say things such as, "It happened so fast. If only I could recapture relationships that I once enjoyed."

Some of us resent dropouts for having left the church, for it seems they are betrayers. Others of us are unwilling to provide the time, patience, and effort that is required to rebuild the bridges.

But our Savior would urge us to minister to dropouts. This is clear in his parable of the lost sheep. Without contemplation, the good shepherd left ninety-nine to locate the one that was lost. And in so doing, he risked his life. When the errant animal was found, there was great rejoicing.[13]

William Barclay makes two important observations concerning this parable that is recorded in Luke 15:

1. There was more rejoicing for the lost that was found than for the never lost (v. 7).

13. According to William Barclay, Judea's shepherd had a very arduous task. Pasture was scarce. The narrow central plateau extended for only a few miles, then plunged down to the jagged cliffs and parched desert. No restraining walls existed, and the sheep could wander.

George Adam Smith wrote of the shepherd: "On some high moor across which at night the hyenas howl, when you meet him, sleepless, far-sighted, weather-beaten, armed, leaning on his staff and looking out over his scattered sheep, every one of them on his heart, you understand why the shepherd of Judea sprang to the front in his people's history; why they gave his name to the kind, and made him the symbol of providence; why Christ took him as the type of self-sacrifice."

The shepherd was personally responsible for his animals. If one was lost, he was required to return the fleece to the owner to reveal how the sheep perished. He was adept at tracking, and could trace a stray's footprints for miles.

Many of the flocks were communal, belonging to entire villages. There would be two or three shepherds in charge. When a sheep was lost, the entire village would be very concerned. Then, when from a distance, they saw the shepherd coming home with the lost sheep across his shoulders, there would be a great shout of thanksgiving. This is the picture that Jesus drew of God, as he responds to one lost sinner returning to the fold.

William Barclay, *Daily Study Bible Series: The Gospel of Luke* (Philadelphia: The Westminster Press, 1953), pp. 206–207.

2. The sheep was lost because of his own foolishness and thoughtlessness, but that didn't cause the shepherd to resent him (v. 5).[14]

The application of these principles to dropouts is clear. But how can we best minister to these wandering sheep?

Researcher and minister John Savage sought answers to this question in the 125 "dropout studies" that he conducted. He discovered these stages that people typically go through when they go from active membership to dropout:

Dropout Stages

1. Faith in spasm

2. Cry for help

3. Anger

4. Limbo

5. Skunk or turtle

6. Sealing off

Ceasing active membership,[15] the potential dropout enters faith in spasm, in which there is a decreased involvement in attendance, commitment, financial contribution, positive attitude, and willingness to articulate his faith. Ninety-five percent of those entering this stage do so because of an anxiety-provoking event.[16]

14. Ibid.

15. In this study, active membership refers to the person who: (1) participates in worship at least 75 percent of the time, excluding summers; (2) has one (or more) commitments such as choir, usher, teacher; (3) makes a financial pledge and pays at least 80 percent of it; (4) has a positive attitude regarding the church; and (5) can articulate the faith that he holds, though perhaps not in an orthodox manner.

16. These four types of anxiety were discovered among the faith-in-spasm people: (1) reality-provoked anxiety: Something happened that created a crisis, and it was witnessed by the person and (or) others. For example, a church leader says, "We must replace you because your Sunday school teaching is inferior." (2) morality-provoked anxiety: An ethical crisis occurred that produces consternation. For example, the choir leader is known

Faith in spasm triggers the doubt mechanism, which pushes the person into stage two: cry for help. This cry is often faint, indirect, impersonal—simply an expression of dislike, such as "Keep treating me this way and I'm leaving."

Ironically, when such cries are heard by persons in the congregation, the response is often critical and defensive. The grapevine goes to work constructing informal systems to screen out such malcontents before they ruin others.

Savage says that between six and ten cries for help are heard each Sunday in the typical church of one hundred. If responded to promptly and appropriately, 98 percent of these members can be salvaged.[17]

The third stage is anger, which the person arrives at when he has reached two conclusions:

1. Nobody *does* hear or help.

2. Nobody *will* hear or help.

At first, such anger is disguised and engulfed in ambivalent language. But before long, it regresses into outright hostility. A rapid change in behavior then occurs: less attendance, less committee work, less involvement in the choir. Finally, the person writes a letter of resignation and stops church affiliation altogether.

---

to be having an affair. (3) neurotically provoked anxiety: Psychic pain is produced through the imagination. For example, due to an overload of responsibilities, the pastor seems to be ignoring the person. He assumes that the pastor no longer likes him. (4) existentially provoked anxiety: This develops when what Tillich terms "awareness of nonbeing" has taken place. There has been a loss of meaning for living. For example, a godly friend dies tragically, and the person concludes that God no longer cares, nor is he fair.

17. These kinds of responses should be given to persons who cry for help: (1) Caring, sensitive persons should be a *perception check*. The crier should be asked a question such as, "Is there something that is making you uncomfortable?" (2) *Listening* to the person's words, but even more to the "throb" of his pain. (3) *Doing something immediately* to assist—even if it is very little. Goal: To communicate that somebody cares. (4) *Revealing your own humanity*, so that the hurting person has somebody to identify with. As one social psychologist suggested, "Misery likes miserable company!"

As a dropout, the individual enters stage four: limbo. He waits, and even hopes, for a visit. He gives the church one last opportunity before closing the door. If no visit occurs, he has a complete change in perspective. That's why this stage is so critical.

During stage five, the dropout becomes either a "skunk" or a "turtle." The former blames external items such as the minister's preaching, and exhibits open criticism. The turtle, by contrast, blames himself, which results in guilt feelings. Skunks feel helpless; turtles sense that they are hopeless.[18]

Stage six involves a sealing-off of emotion from the church, a pervasive feeling of indifference. This is accompanied by a reinvestment of time and energy into other commitments. Once a person becomes entrenched in this new perspective for four months, Savage says, the task of getting him to return is exceedingly difficult.

But all hope is not vanished. Rescue is yet possible if the right approach is used. Over 63 percent of the dropouts visited by persons trained by the researcher *did* return—and after just *one* visit.

What specific skills and attitudes did they use? The same ones we must employ if we expect to reach these isolated persons. They are as follows:

1. Recognize that dropouts often have serious family problems. Be prepared for shocking revelations, as well as hidden messages.

2. Do not go to tell but to listen. Dropouts have waited long to pour out their ideas and feelings to persons who truly care enough to listen.

3. Be very patient. There will be no quick fix. Rebuilding confidence is a gradual, time-and-energy-

---

18. As an addendum, the researcher explains that "skunks" tend to marry "turtles." And sometimes "turtles" marry "turtles." But rarely do "skunks" marry "skunks."

Also, it is a fact that most ministers tend to be turtlelike. That is why they often hesitate to make calls on dropouts. It makes them feel guilty and responsible.

consuming process. In the words of Savage, "Sheep get lost blade-by-blade. They nibble themselves lost, and they must return the same way."

4. The church body must be prepared to welcome these persons once they return. Total forgiveness. Quickly reknit friendships. Immediate involvement in responsibilities. And most crucial of all, a complete absence of screening systems that demand penance, open confession, and a demonstration of worth.

It must not be assumed that all dropouts have turned their backs on God. Some have been unjustly treated by laymen or pastors in the church. In such cases, apologies are essential, followed by complete acceptance.[19]

No ministry lies closer to the heart of the good shepherd than that to lost sheep. It's time that we his followers adopt the same priority.

Singles and dropouts. Persons who, for whatever reason, have become distant from the church. We must go to them with open, sensitive, and compassionate hearts. It is what our Lord does and what he expects of us.

The End of Two Romances

I wish that you could have known her when she was young, vibrant, very much in love with her new husband —as well as with her growing, caring church. She spoke freely of spiritual things. Of God's goodness. Of her closeness with Christian brothers and sisters.

Then came a multiplicity of explosions in rapid succession. The news that she had an incurable disease. The discovery that her husband was seeing another woman. The suspicions from church members she had trusted very much. The pastor who somehow became too uncon-

19. The John Savage material was extracted from a videotape presentation, "The Dropout Track." For more information about these study materials, or the John Savage seminars, please contact: L. E. A. D. Consultants, Incorporated, Post Office Box 664, Reynoldsburg, Ohio 43068. Telephone (614) 864-0156.

cerned to respond to her. Like the Tacoma bridge, all the crosswinds converged to result in her sudden collapse.

Her response, like Job's, was predictable: "Why me, Lord? What have I possibly done to deserve this?"

Then came the formal split of her marriage, followed by her husband's unwillingness to provide for her care as the court had ordered. Have you heard the expression "hung out to dry?"

It was then that this broken young lady turned off completely. She decided to break all ties with church people. After all, they had forsaken her when she needed them most. Instead of compassion, all they could give her was a suspicious look and unfair judgment. Why should she subject herself to such punishment?

Cherry and I have continued to befriend her since she dropped out. Little by little she has begun to melt. She has even attended a few church services on special occasions.

Nevertheless, our friend remains distant. From the church. And far worse, from Jesus Christ.

We'll continue to try. Miracles are possible. We hope for one to soon occur.

But, while reaching out in love, our minds continue to focus on the lack of loving response that put her in this sad state. Loyal, regularly attending church persons failed to reach out. To them she was an expendable casualty.

It is crucial that we clearly see that, in the eyes of Jesus, there is no such person!

Neglecting One, We Neglect All

Section Two of this book focuses on four distinct kinds of people. People to whom we as followers of the master must build bridges.

As we have seen, different approaches are required for each bridge type. Our preparation for these varied challenges will require learning in our heads as well as in our hearts. Few of us have mastered the necessary skills and attitudes.

Many of us are quite content to reach out to our favorite kind of people. We're intent on being relationship specialists. Somehow, we feel that this is sufficient.

The Savior sees it differently. He says that it is his will that *all* should come to repentance (2 Peter 3:9). When it comes to his loving acceptance of mankind, he is certainly no specialist. His grace is so abundant and indiscriminate. He knows that by slighting one, he would be neglecting all. Likewise, we as his followers dare not be selective.

Section One admonishes us to construct our bridges in skillful, correct ways so that they are sound and reliable. Section Two appeals to us to build a variety of bridges that extend to a diversity of people.

Section Three, to which we now turn, focuses on what our bridges should transport once they are in place. To make them reliable and extend them to worthy destinations is not enough. The purpose of our bridges is to allow necessary goods to be delivered. Spiritual commerce must take place.

What goods are we referring to? The life-giving fruit of the Spirit. Let's taste and see that they are good.

Part **3**

Bridges/Delivery
Holy Relationships

Today you will meet all kinds of unpleasant people; they will hurt you, injure you and insult you; but you cannot live like that; you know better, for you are a man in whom the (S)pirit of God dwells.—Roman Emperor, Marcus Aurelius, to his son

Society is the walls of our imprisonment in history —Peter Berger

Just because you're not paranoid doesn't mean the world is not out to get you.

9

Fruit Cluster #1: Love, Joy, Peace

Cultivating healthy and holistic relationships prepares us for the main event—creating ones that are holy. Ones that free us to become delivery systems of Christ's love.

Construction is complete. Our tall, stalwart bridges are custom designed for the four kinds of persons we will (or should) encounter.

Now it's time to begin transporting our spiritual fruit across the bridges, all nine varieties itemized in Galatians 5:22–23: "love, joy, peace, patience, kindness, goodness, faithfulness, gentleness and self-control."[1]

1. The "prince of expositors," Alexander Maclaren, notes that Paul refers to fruit, not fruits. Thus, "all this rich variety of graces, of conduct and character, is [to be] thought of as one." He continues by saying, "The individual members are not isolated graces, but all connected, springing from one root and constituting an organic whole."

The works of the flesh have no such unity (i.e., not worthy to be termed fruit). Alexander Maclaren, *Expositions of Holy Scripture: Second Corinthians, Galatians and*

161

Here are some basic principles related to these life-giving fruit.

First, love should be perceived as the super fruit. Some suggest that the other eight are hybrids, or derivatives, of love. Others see love as the life sap that rises through the tree, giving sustenance and form to the other fruit. Both viewpoints have merit.

The fruit of the Spirit increase and decrease together, just like the water levels in the battery cells of my car. Thus, when we mature in patience, we also grow in joy and peace.

Second, the fruit of the Spirit always comes in a package that includes all nine. When we purchase ice cream bars at the grocery store, we can't usually buy just one or two. We're required to take the whole box. Similarly, as Christians we must buy into all nine fruit. It's a simple case of all or nothing, feast or famine, abundance or destitute poverty.

Finally, the fruit is not optional for those of us who love the Lord. Jesus made this clear in his farewell message on the eve of his crucifixion.

> I am the vine; you are the branches. If a man remains in me and I in him, he will bear much fruit.... You did not choose me, but I chose you...to go and bear fruit—fruit that will last (John 15:5, 16).

If this is all true, why do we not hear more about the fruit of the Spirit? Because we hear so much about the gifts of the Spirit.

Philippians (New York: Hodder and Stoughton—George H. Doran Company, n.d.) pp. 162–163.

Another interesting perspective is presented by Jim Elliot "Rot will encourage rot, but one ripe piece of fruit will not allay rottenness in another." Implication: Fruit exist in unity. One piece that goes bad can make others distasteful. However, the reverse is not true. A good piece cannot make one that's gone bad better. "The Journals of Jim Elliot," *Christianity Today*, November 21, 1986, page titled "Classic and Contemporary Excerpts," p. 25.

To Be or to Do?

Author Donald Cole is right. Christians today seem obsessed with the gifts of the Holy Spirit. Perhaps it's because they are more observable. More closely related to our insatiable craving to perform. To do wonders and be seen while doing them. Having a bunch of gifts allows us to be ostentatious.

Or, it could be that compared with the fruit of the Spirit, spiritual gifts are more spectacular. The latter are more like the ocean's rip-tide, while the former resemble the sea's hidden, silent current. We gravitate to the spectacular. The sensational. Just as did those who harassed Jesus to perform nonstop miracles.

Certainly, the gifts get an inordinate amount of press— compared with the fruit.

Admittedly, Paul mentions such gifts (Rom. 12:3–8; 1 Cor. 12—14; Eph. 4:7–16).[2] Yet, they pale in significance when contrasted with the fruit.

Everything that Paul says about spiritual gifts centers on one thing: holy living. On bearing fruit of the Spirit in our lives.

2. Kenneth Kinghorn has summarized the gifts of the Spirit on this helpful chart. From *Gifts of the Spirit* (Abingdon Press, 1976).

Romans 12:6–8	1 Corinthians 12:4–11	1 Corinthians 12:28	Ephesians 4:11
Prophecy	Prophecy	Prophecy	Prophecy
Teaching		Teaching	Teaching
Serving			
Exhortation			
Leadership			
Giving Aid			
Compassion			
	Healing	Healing	
	Working miracles	Working miracles	
	Tongues and their interpretation	Tongues and their interpretation	
	Wisdom		
	Knowledge		
	Faith		
	Discernment		
		Apostleship	Apostleship
		Helps	
		Administration	
			Evangelism
			Shepherding

His conclusion must be the same as our own. Our gifts profit nil if we lack the Son-ripened fruit of holiness in our lives (1 Cor. 13).

Gifts can be faked. Phonies can learn to preach like prophets—TV evangelists notwithstanding. As Cole says, "Convincing pretenses can counterfeit giftedness."

Not so with Christian fruit. They cannot be feigned. The quality of their harvest gives them away. James says so.

> But the wisdom that comes from heaven is . . . pure; then peaceloving, considerate, submissive, full of mercy and good fruit, impartial and sincere. Peacemakers who sow in peace raise a harvest of righteousness (3:17–18).

For any of us who might be tempted to become spiritual fruit impostors, Jesus says,

> By [your] fruit [I] will recognize [you]. Do people pick grapes from thornbushes, or figs from thistles? Likewise every good tree bears good fruit, but a bad tree bears bad fruit. A good tree cannot bear bad fruit, and a bad tree cannot bear good fruit (Matt. 7:16–18).

Here is a final, essential contrast between gifts and fruit. The former diminish in effectiveness through time. The curve ball of poor health, as well as the church's moth-ball mentality regarding its aged, take their toll.

By contrast, the older we get, the more fruit should be expected in our lives. Cole reflects the sentiments of many of us when he says, "Nothing is sweeter than Christlike character in aging people." Why? Because it gives all of us hope for our own future. Someday, we can be that way, too. And in the meantime, we can work, toward that idea.

In summary, there's no contest. Fruit is more important than gifts, in spite of what we're likely to hear.[3]

---

3. "Opinion: To Be or to Do?" *Moody Monthly*, September, 1983, p. 17.

But if fruit outshine gifts, they don't even deserve to be compared with sins. Paul does so anyway, just to tell us how good we have it.

Beware of the Briar Patch!

In Galatians 5:19–21 Paul writes,

> The acts of the sinful nature are obvious: sexual immorality, impurity and debauchery; idolatry and witchcraft; hatred, discord, jealousy, fits of rage, selfish ambition, dissensions, factions and envy; drunkenness, orgies, and the like. I warn you . . . those who live like this will not inherit the kingdom of God.

The list of losers has been called the misery index. As with the fruit, all of these come—and go—in a package. They are inseparable.

By making this contrast, Paul provides a classic statement concerning the inner strife between spirit and flesh.[4] The first causes us to bear fruit; the second produces thorns of sin.

That strife is ended when our sinful nature is crucified[5] (Gal. 2:20; 5:24;[6] Rom. 6:6). As Lamar Kincaid vividly

---

4. W. T. Purkiser declares that the Galatians 5 contains a classic statement related to "flesh-Spirit" inner strife. Along with Romans 7, it has been taken as normative for the highest Christian life. "For the sinful nature (Gr., *sarx*; flesh, KJV, RSV) desires what is contrary to the Spirit, and the Spirit what is contrary to the sinful nature." The *sarx*, or "sinful nature" here doesn't imply bodily or physical as do the acts of sin that are listed. W. T. Purkiser, *Exploring Christian Holiness: The Biblical Foundation*, Volume I (Beacon Hill Press of Kansas City, 1983), p. 166.

5. Raymond T. Stamm writes: "Crucifixion with Christ means three things. a) Participation in the benefits of Christ's death, including freedom from law, forgiveness for past sins, and a passionate urge never to sin again (Rom. 4:24–25; 2 Cor. 5:14–15, 20; Col. 3:1–4). b) A moral, spiritual fellowship with Christ in his death and resurrection, which takes the Christian's "I will" captive to "the mind of Christ," replacing the law as a design for living (2 Cor. 10:3–6; Phil. 3:10; Rom. 6:1–11). c) A partnership with Christ in his creative suffering, which requires the Christian to "complete what remains of Christ's afflictions" for the sake of his body the church (Col. 1:24–25; 3:5; Rom. 8:17)." *The Interpreter's Bible*, Volume 10 (Abingdon Press), p. 489.

6. In Galatians 5:24, the crucifixion is "the sinful nature with its passions and desires." Such a crucifixion relates to "those who belong to Christ Jesus." Belonging to Jesus in its

declared, we must "ruthlessly nail our sinful nature to the hard wood [of the cross] with resolute, unrelenting blows; and like the crucifixion squad [that slew our Lord], we must sit and watch it with hard eyes, wither and plead how it may, until it dies."[7]

It is as simple as this. When our sinful nature dies with Jesus on the cross, he becomes resurrected in us through his abiding Spirit. And what evidence do we possess that this miracle has occurred? His fruit exhibited in our lives. We become spiritual fruit vendors!

With this background in mind, we're now ready to examine the nine fruit. We will be focusing on them in groups of three.[8] The first group—love, joy, and peace—have to do with our relationship with our heavenly Father and the resulting renewal of our inner life.

Let's begin with love.

The World's Best Four-letter Word

Aldous Huxley stated that the word *love* is bankrupt. "Of all the worn, smudged, dog-eared words in our vocabulary, *love* is the grubbiest." Yet most people prefer thinking about this term more than all others.

---

full scope involves these three states. 1) *We are Christ's by creation—he made us;* 2) *We are Christ's by the cross, by redemption—he purchased us;* 3) *We are Christ's by consecration—the self-yielding of those already "alive from the dead"* (Rom. 6:13 kjv). Purkiser, op. cit., p. 167.

7. Lamar Kincaid, in a sermon preached at Longboat Key Chapel, Longboat Key, Florida, 1973.

Just as Romans 7:14–25 must be interpreted in harmony with its context in Romans 6 and 8, so Galatians 5:17 must be interpreted in harmony with verse 24. The inner strife—so far as "sinful nature" is concerned—is concluded when it is crucified. To see crucifixion as a gradual, continual dying that never results in death is to miss the biblical and natural meaning of the term. Thus, our death to self comes at one point in time. Ibid.

8. It is probable that Paul did not have well-tailored triads in mind when he listed the fruit of the Spirit. But, for purposes of conceptualizing, we follow Alexander Maclaren's lead in doing so. Admittedly, this categorization seems to be more forced than those traditional ones that have grouped the Beatitudes and Ten Commandments. Nevertheless, we shall do so anyhow.

Maclaren, in making his classification, states, "It is perhaps not too artificial to point out that we have three triads, of which the first describes the life of the Spirit in its deepest secret; the second, the same life in its manifestations to men; and the third, that life in relation to the difficulties of the world, and of ourselves." Maclaren, *op. cit.*, p. 163.

In a secular sense, the word *love* is used a million different ways,[9] the first meaning that comes to mind for most people is love between the sexes. In contrast to infatuation, love is often more realistic, as reflected in this viewpoint:

> Infatuation is when you think he's as handsome as Robert Redford, as smart as Henry Kissinger, as noble as Ralph Nader, as funny as Woody Allen, and as athletic as Jimmy Connors. Love is when you realize that he's as handsome as Woody Allen, as smart as Jimmy Connors, as funny as Ralph Nader, as athletic as Henry Kissinger, and nothing like Robert Redford—but you'll take him anyway![10]

Is there more to love than infatuation from a secular perspective? Psychologist Robert Trotter states that love has three sides, like a triangle.

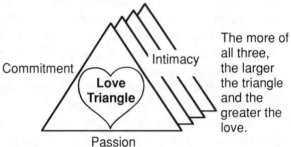

The more of all three, the larger the triangle and the greater the love.

9. According to J. A. M. Meerloo, the phrase "I love you" can be: (1) a stage song, repeated daily without any meaning; (2) a barely audible murmur, full of surrender; (3) a statement that means "I desire you," "I want you sexually," "I hope you love me," or "I hope that I will be able to love you"; (4) a phrase that often means "It may be that a love relationship can be developed between us"; (5) a wish for emotional exchange: "I want your admiration in exchange for mine," or "I give my love in exchange for some passion," or "I want to feel cozy and at home with you," or "I admire some of your qualities"; (6) a deep, intimate request: "I desire you," or "I want you to gratify me," or "I want your protection," or "I want to be intimate with you," or "I want to exploit your loveliness"; (7) a need for security and tenderness—for parental treatment; (8) an expression of submissiveness: "Please take me as I am," or "I feel guilty about you"; (9) a self-sacrifice and masochistic wish for dependency—or a full affirmation of the other, taking the responsibility for mutual exchange of feelings; (10) a weak feeling of friendliness—or the scarcely-whispered expression of ecstasy.

"I love you"—wish, desire, submission, conquest. It is never the word itself that tells the real meaning." *Conversation and Communication*

10. *Redbook*, February, 1975.

Commitment is the mental component of love. It's what some couples have left after intimacy is lost and passion has subsided.

Intimacy, says Trotter, is the emotional side of love. Some can bare their souls to one another, but have little commitment or passion. Theirs is a high-grade friendship.

Passion is the motivational aspect of love. When it alone rules, there may be an affair in which there is little intimacy and even less commitment. This is the infatuation described above.[11]

Christian love, indeed, includes commitment, intimacy, and passion. Nevertheless, Christian love goes beyond the world's ideas of love: the brotherly, erotic, and other kinds that the ancient Greeks described.[12]

Christian love is agape, the love we extend to all people, the God-breathed love that permeates our being when his Spirit inhabits our hearts. It is unconditional (given without its recipient having to earn it or live down the past); unselfish (accompanied by a willingness to suffer for the beloved); unrestricted (available to everyone, especially the unlovely and unlovable).

How does Christian love penetrate our lives? By our relinquishing our will to the will of Jesus. To quote Paul Ramsey, it has "nothing to do with feelings, emotions, taste, preferences, temperament, or any of the qualities in

11. Robert J. Trotter, "The Three Faces of Love," *Psychology Today* (September, 1986), pp. 46–54.

12. In Greek there are four different words for "love." (1) *Storge*, which implies family love, the love of a parent for a child and vice versa. "Sweet is a father to his children if he has *storge*." (2) *Eros*, which describes the love of a man for a woman—passionate and sexual love. Nothing immoral is necessarily implied, but through time it has taken on the implication of lust. (3) *Philia*, which describes warm, tender affection—the kind that exists between close friends. Hence, the name "Philadelphia," the city of brotherly love." (4) *Agape*, which means "unconquerable benevolence, invincible good will." It does not mean a feeling of the heart, which we cannot help; it means a "determination of the mind" and will toward those who are unlovely. We can only have *agape* when Jesus helps us to conquer our natural tendency to anger and bitterness.

William Barclay, *The Daily Study Bible: The Gospel of Matthew*, Volume 1 (Philadelphia: The Westminster Press, 1956), pp. 172–173. Most Christians call John the Apostle of love, but Paul used the term *agape* seventy-five times. John's Gospel only employs it seven, while his First Epistle uses it another eighteen times.

other people that arouse feelings of revulsion or attraction, negative or positive preferences. Christian love depends on the direction of the will...not on stirring emotion.[13]

The Bible is replete with words about the love that characterizes us as Christians. It is

a prize to be won. 1 Corinthians 14:1 instructs us to "follow the way of love." The Greek word for "follow" implies a strenuous activity. Paul translates the same word "press," in Philippians 3:14 KJV: "I press toward the mark...of the high calling of God in Christ Jesus."

an object of prayer. Paul says, "And this I pray, that your love may abound yet more and more. "(Phil. 1:9, KJV). The term *abound* comes from the Latin word that means "overflowing like the breaking waves of the sea."

a model to be followed. 1 John 4:19 declares, "We love because he first loved us." As Reuben Welch likes to say, "When we think of love, color it Jesus."

The great symphony of love is located in the thirteenth chapter of 1 Corinthians. Fifteen beautiful refrains blend perfectly into a rhapsody of splendor.

Love is patient	Love is not self-seeking	Love protects
Love is kind	Love is not easily	Love trusts
Love does not	angered	Love hopes
envy	Love keeps no record of	Love endures
Love does not	wrongs	Love never fails
boast or is not	Love does not delight in	(verses 4–8a)
proud	evil	
Love is not rude	Love rejoices with the	
	truth	

Charles Swindoll summarized these spectacular char-

13. Quoted by J. Glenn Gould in "Neighborly Love in the Christian Life," Herald of Holiness, April 1, 1987, p. 7.

acteristics of Christian love into five statements. He terms them the *ABCs of love*.

> I *A*ccept you as you are.
> I *B*elieve you are valuable.
> I *C*are when you hurt.
> I *D*esire only what is best for you.
> I *E*rase all offenses.[14]

This kind of loving spirit is bound to penetrate the lives of all we encounter, as does salt, light, and leaven. I can't help thinking of a custom of an African tribe. Whenever someone does something vile and unlawful, he is required to stand in the center of a circle that is formed by all members of the group. While there, he must listen to and look into the eyes of each person, who in turn explains why he still loves him.

The effect is amazing. He leaves, that day, determined to rise to the level of the others' expectation. To never disappoint those who love him so deeply, again. To begin loving with the same kind of love that he has generously received.

No matter what we do, Jesus loves us without limit or reservation. As Karl Barth once said, the greatest truth in God's Word is this: "Jesus loves me, this I know, for the Bible tells me so."

Whenever we falter and stumble, whether by wickedness or by weariness, he looks straight into our eyes and says, "I love you." That should be enough to make us, like the Africans, love everyone with the same kind of love that Jesus gives us.

Color It Orange

Orange is my favorite color. So alive. So vibrant. So pulsating with energy.

But not just any shade of orange will do. It must be

---

14. Charles R. Swindoll, *Dropping Your Guard: The Value of Open Relationships* (Waco, TX: Word Books, 1983), p. 122

bright like a Popsicle, a freshly peeled carrot, or the swing set in the city park.

If joy is a spiritual fruit, I like to think of it as orange— bright orange. Like the Golden Gate on a sunny day, gleaming on San Francisco's skyline, guarding the sparkling, azure waters below.

Don't expect to read about joy in a psychology textbook or a philosophy treatise. It's purely a Christian attitude. And that is why it appears nearly two hundred times in God's Word.

We read that angels brought "good tidings of great joy" when they announced our Savior's birth (Luke 2:10 KJV). Later, Jesus declared the purpose of his teaching to be "my joy . . . in you, and . . . your joy . . . full" (John 15:11 KJV).

Our only source of authentic joy is Christ. With comforting assurance we sing

> If you want joy,
>   real joy,
>   wonderful joy.
> Let Jesus come into
>   you heart.[15]

We must not get confused. Joy is not the same as fun. The kind purchased at Disneyland or a World Series game.

Nor is it like happiness, which depends on favorable outward circumstances.

Rather, joy is strictly an inside job! It is generated from the wellsprings of our souls when our souls have been touched by God.

For this reason we Christians can be joyful even when things appear dark, dismal, destitute, and depressing. When fun and happiness make their exit, joy can linger.

Joy causes us to be a blessing to those in need. We encourage others by being joyful. Also, it grounds us in

15. "If You Want Joy," author unknown.

the will of God. He is pleased when our cups are full and running over. Finally, joy yields plenty of personal satisfaction and fulfillment. It adds zest to our lives. As Charles Swindoll said, too many go around looking like their rich aunt just willed her millions to her pregnant hamster!

Once Christ's joy floods our hearts, how should we best use it to his glory? The Bible clearly instructs us.

1. Do something for and in the Name of our Lord. His disciples did so, and "returned again with joy" (Luke 10:17 KJV).

2. Freely ask and generously receive from the hands of Christ. He instructed: "Ask and ye shall receive, that your joy may be full" (John 16:24 KJV).

3. Close the book on devastating memories and crippling resentments. After enduring great persecution, Paul and Barnabas were "filled with joy" (Acts 13:52).

4. With divine guidance, learn to cope with life's constant stresses. James admonished: "Reckon it nothing but joy whenever you find yourselves surrounded by various temptations" (James 1:2, Weymouth).

Like love, joy is God's free gift to us, although it cost him plenty. It is a fruit that we can possess that will make our lives fulfilling. With it, we are soaring eagles. Without it, we are little more than worms on a hangglider.

Prior to becoming a minister, my dad, like his father, worked in the coal mines of southern Illinois. One day I heard him recall how black soot would blanket everything nearby.

But it always used to intrigue him how lilies never had a speck of coal dust on their petals. They could be located right next to the cave entrance. Still they remain unblemished.

Out of curiosity, one day my father investigated how this occurred. What he discovered taught him an interesting thing about nature, but an even more valuable lesson about the Christian life.

He learned that lilies continuously excrete a cleansing solution. The petals are thus bathed so that the irritating and unpleasant-looking soot rolls right off.

Joy is like lilies. Because of the presence of Jesus within, our spirit is continually vitalized and encouraged. Although Satan's "coal dust" of disappointment, evil, and confusion may come our way, it cannot attach itself to our inner spirits. Joy is like having perpetual windshield wipers on our hearts.

Again, joy keeps us spiritually upbeat regardless of anything this world can throw in our direction, or, for that matter, anything other Christians can lob our way. Christians? You bet. They can be pain inflicting. One bumper sticker captured this sentiment: "The more Christians I know, the more I like my dog!"

Granted. It shouldn't be that way. Our brothers and sisters in Christ should soothe our spirits. To paraphrase Tom Dooley, they should be "comforting the afflicted" not "afflicting the comforted."

But having said that, it is just as certain that we should still remain joyful. Just as the early Christians did in the midst of intense persecution. In describing their jubilant spirits, the Bible employs a term from which we derive our word *hilarious*.

Rather than succumbing to depression or fear, they delighted in being together with hilarity and celebration. Their churches exuded joy.

We should be doing the same. So here's my challenge: Let's begin immediately to wash off the coal dust!

No More Inner Rumble

If joy is orange, peace must be white. Again, lilies come to mind, the kind that fill cemeteries. Then there is the white dove. With the traditional olive branch in his mouth, he becomes the international symbol of peace. Finally, there is the white flag, signifying that hostilities have ceased and a truce has begun.

This statement will not surprise you: Our world lacks peace. Throughout recorded history, there have only been two hundred years when fighting had altogether ceased. And most of the war years have featured multiple conflicts going on simultaneously.

But conflict, certainly, is not limited to battlefields "over there." We have plenty right here at home. Married couples do battle with words, withdrawal, and physical weapons. I heard about one fellow who went to a restaurant, called the waitress over, and said, "Serve me cold eggs and burnt toast. Then, while I eat it, stand here and nag me. I'm homesick!"

Our children aren't exempt from conflict. Cartoons feature a blow a minute. I think the Roadrunner deserves the Congressional Medal of Honor. The poor fellow gets pulverized every five seconds.

We encourage our children to think in this direction. Not only do we model warfare in our marriages, but we purchase them the latest toy weapons of aggression. I had to smile when I saw this account of a request made to Santa last Christmas:

> **Santa**: Ho, ho, ho. Hello there, young fellow. Isn't this a wonderful time of the year? We're celebrating peace on earth, goodwill to men! Now, what would you like for Christmas?
> **Boy**: A death-ray laser zap gun, a toy electric chair, and a chainsaw murderer doll.

Nevertheless, deep down, we all see the value of peace. As in the days of Jeremiah, we cry out. "Peace, peace... [but] there is no peace" (6:14). Overt, as well as covert, conflict continues. Between nations. Between individuals. At work. On highways. In our homes. Even in our churches—where we're supposed to be honoring the Prince of Peace.

But we must focus on the Bible's view of peace, which contrasts sharply with the world's limited understanding of the concept.

According to William Barclay, the Greek term for *peace (eirene)* corresponds with the Hebrew word *shalom* that we're more familiar with. Rather than simply implying a freedom from trouble, it means a serene heart which results from the all-pervading consciousness that our lives are in God's hands.[16]

Paul used the term *peace* forty-three times. He treasured the concept, and rarely omitted it from his salutations. Repeatedly, we read "Grace to you and peace" (Rom. 1:7).

But what did he and other Bible writers declare about peace? Three main things.

First, Jesus is its source. In Ephesians, we're told that Christ's atonement brings us peace. "For he himself is our peace" (2:14). Just before ascending into heaven, he testified to the same reality. "Peace I leave with you; my peace I give you" (John 14:27).

We're tempted to set our minds on other sources as we grope for peace. On ourselves—which yields conceit or depression. On circumstances—which results in false security or broken dreams. On things—which invite slavery or total frustration. On people—which encourages idol worship or causes shattered spirits.

Again, we must look to Jesus. For, in him, we are guaranteed a deep, authentic peace. A peace which "transcends all understanding" of this world (Phil. 4:7).

Second, having the peace of Jesus within, we're at peace with his heavenly Father, others, and ourselves.

The Greek word for *peace* includes a root that means "to join or set at one." Christ's peace results in our being in harmony with God. And, as one person rightly de-

16. William Barclay, op. cit., *The Letters to the Galatians and Ephesians*, p. 55.

clared, "We can't possibly experience the peace *of* God until we're at peace *with* God."

Jesus makes it possible to be just that. Romans 5:1 says so. "Therefore, since we have been justified through faith, we have peace with God through our Lord Jesus Christ."

His peace also helps us to be at peace with others. As the chorus says, "He is our peace, who has broken down every wall."[17] The Bible, similarly, says, For he himself is our peace, who has made the two [Jew and Gentile] one and has destroyed the barrier, the dividing wall of hostility (Eph. 2:14).

Because he has made the gift of peace possible, his Word commands us to activate it in our lives and to become peacemakers.[18]

Finally, the peace of God provided by his Son our Savior makes us at peace within ourselves. Peace like a river floods our hearts and lives, just as Isaiah the prophet predicted. "Thou wilt keep him in perfect peace, *whose* mind *is* stayed *on thee:* because he trusteth in thee" (26:3 KJV).

Many of us have an acute case of the jitters. We nail bite our way through life, fearing everything that moves. We're so paranoid that our fears have fears.

J. L. Glass has written a humorous article, titled "Five Ways to Have a Nervous Breakdown." He lists them as follows:

1. Try to figure out the answer before the problem arises. "Most of the bridges we cross are never built, because they are unnecessary." We carry tomorrow's load along with today's. Matthew 6:34 says: "Do not worry about tomorrow, for tomorrow will worry about itself."

17. "He Has Broken Down Every Wall," Kandela Groves, Maranatha Music, 1975.
18. See Matthew 5:9, 10:34; Mark 9:50; Romans 12:18, 14:19; 2 Corinthians 13:11; 1 Thessalonians 5:13.

2. Try to relive the past. As we trust him for the future, we must trust him with the past. And he can use the most checkered past imaginable for his good. See Romans 8:28.

3. Try to avoid making decisions. Doing this is like deciding whether to allow weeds to grow in our gardens. While we're deciding, they're growing. Decisions will be made in our delay. We must come to grips with the realities of life. Choice "is man's most godlike characteristic."

4. Demand more of yourself than you can produce. Unrealistic demands result in "beating our heads against stone walls. We don't change the walls. We just damage ourselves." Romans 12:3 says, "Do not think of yourself more highly than you ought, but rather think of yourself with sober judgment."

5. Believe everything Satan tells you. The New Testament speaks of the "devices of the devil" (Eph. 6:11, NEB). Jesus described Satan as the "father of lies" (John 8:44). He's a master of disguise, masquerading as an angel of light. But our Lord declared *that his* sheep follow him because they "know His voice" (John 10:4). Why? They have listened to it in his Word.[19]

We need to replace these foolish prescriptions with Christ's abiding peace placed in our hearts by his Spirit, so that we can sing, "It is well with my soul" and really mean it.

His peace does wonderful things for us. It causes us to love his law (Ps. 119:165), be protected (Luke 19:41–42), quiet, and assured (Isa. 32:17). As a result, we need not be anxious over anything (Phil. 4:6–7)—even death.

---

19. Quoted by W. T. Purkiser in "Five Ways to Have a Nervous Breakdown," *Herald of Holiness*, October 9, 1974.

General Booth, godly founder of the Salvation Army, lay dying. He seemed to glow with God's presence. All of a sudden he seemed to grimace with pain.

One of his dear friends, standing by his bedside, leaned down and whispered, "Tell me how you feel, my brother." With a very weak voice, the saint said, "The waters are rising."

But then, in a voice almost too weak to be heard, he muttered, "But, praise Jesus, I am rising with the waters."

Inner peace does that, you know. With it filling our hearts, we will rise with the waters of life, no matter how cold, how high, how rapid.

To reiterate, Paul is absolutely right in telling us:

> Do not be anxious about anything, but in everything, by prayer and petition, with thanksgiving, present your requests to God. And the peace of God, which transcends all understanding, will guard your hearts and your minds in Christ Jesus (Phil 4:6–7).

Love. Joy. Peace. All are intimately involved in our Christian walk. And all are possible only because of our relationship with Christ.

Let's turn our attention to the next three fruit. They follow the first three in logical order. Because of love, joy, and peace within, we are now prepared for patience, kindness, and goodness.

To live above with those we love,
  oh that will be glory;
But to live below with those we know,
  that's another story.

The best relations are built up, like fine lacquer finish, with accumulated layers of acts of kindness.—Alan McGinnis

The shortest possible fragment of time: between the time when the traffic light changes and the person behind you honks.

10

Fruit Cluster #2: Patience, Kindness, Goodness

In addition to our first cart of fruit—love, joy, and peace—there is a second that contains patience, kindness, and goodness. Let's load it for immediate delivery over our bridges.

As we have stated, the first triad primarily involves our intimacy with God. The second concerns our relationships with others, particularly those who are close up. Those we frequently interact with eyeball-to-eyeball. Family members. Work colleagues. Fellow parishioners.

We know the kind. They are persons we feel an emotional attachment to, but, they are also ones who have the potential of really getting on our nerves. Why? Because we're so close to them that their bad days become our bad days.

From our vantage point, these are the persons whom we tend to take for granted. We expect them to come

179

through for us, just as they always have. When they do, we offer them few, if any, thank yous or strokes. They only hear from us when they fail to meet our level of expectations.

What does this cluster of fruit have to do with the one that we loaded onto the first cart? More than we can possibly realize. Closeness with God implies a sense of oneness with others.

Theologian Martin Buber put it succinctly. He said that when our relationship with God changes from "I-It" (impersonal) to "I-Thou" (intimate)—as evidenced by his Spirit's love, joy, and peace in our lives—our associations with others take on a new and fulfilling dimension.[1]

My good friend David Best stated the same fact in a recent sermon. He said when we become dependent upon God, we'll find ourselves becoming increasingly independent of the past (guilt, painful memories) and interdependent with others.

It's fruit inspection time. Let's begin investigating this cluster by focusing on the fruit of patience.

And I Want It Right Now!

Here are some things that drive me right up the wall:

Putting a complicated gadget together—especially when the instructions don't make sense.

Getting through to someone who is carrying on a telephone marathon—especially when, after finally getting through, I get a recording.

Investing loyalty in a team (e.g., Dodgers) whose percentage of losses matches southern California's July temperature—especially when I hear reports of dissension among players.

---

1. Martin Buber, *I and Thou* (New York: Scribner, 1958).

Missing the green light because the driver in the car ahead of me is distracted—especially when *that* bozo makes the light.

We can all envision similar scenes that make our blood pressures rise, our heads ache, and our teeth grind. Who needs that kind of hassle, especially those of us who have type A (antsy) personalities?

What makes it particularly difficult is the fact that so many *others* are impatient, too. As Howard White once remarked, "I'm not sure whether the rat race is speeding up, or if they're just bringing on faster rats." Both seem to be true. And, the rats appear to be increasingly impatient.

Some of us might be saying to ourselves, "But our inner feeling of impatience motivates us to perform." Marchant King concurs by saying, "Impatience is the spur that motivates progress in modern business. The corporation that 'can't wait until tomorrow' is likely to become the most successful in its field."[2]

To procrastinate is indeed to fail. Like the old blacksmith, we must strike while the iron's hot. And impatience may help us to do just that.

Nevertheless, being prompt need not be the result of such a negative motivation. We can be patient and prompt, too, and as a result have the best of both worlds. We must not think of patience as synonymous with procrastination.

Our Bible is replete with references concerning patience. The Greek term *makrothumia* (translated "long-suffering," KJV), means "not being quickly or easily provoked by the unsatisfactory conduct of others." Or, as nineteenth-century Anglican Bishop J. B. Lightfoot said, it is the "self-restraint that does not hastily retaliate a wrong."[3]

2. Marchant A. King, "Patience," *Moody Monthly*, September, 1983, p. 23.

3. Ibid. Also, William Barclay, *The Daily Study Bible: The Letters to the Galatians and Ephesians* (Philadelphia, PA: The Westminster Press, 1954.)

But, what is considered a wrong tends to differ between non-Christians and those of us who love the Lord.

The unregenerated are more quickly set off by persons who sorely inconvenience them. Persons who block their personal needs and ambitions. In effect, they say, "I'll be nice, provided others don't cross me. If they do, they've got problems." It's the old don't-rattle-my-cage syndrome.

Unfortunately, some of us who have been born again react similarly. But we know better and usually feel guilty when we stoop to such attitudes and behavior.

We're more likely to become impatient with persons who fail Jesus. Persons whose lives don't match their testimonies. Persons who hurt Christ's kingdom (intentionally or not) by acting stupidly, stubbornly, or sinfully.

Also, we tend to chafe when others don't move with dispatch, especially when they're sluggardly and slothful and the needs are intense but "the workers are few" (Matt. 9:37). Those of us who want to see miraculous things happen, because God has given us this vision, tend to lose our cool around sleepy-eyed saints.

But, as the writer to the Hebrews declares, "[We] have need of patience" (10:36, KJV). And we have it for two important reasons.

First, patience will help us to persevere. To persevere means to put up with a lot of stuff that we don't deserve. Taking our licks because of our mistakes is not especially commendable, but our enduring blows that are unfairly given us is meritorious with God. 1 Peter 2:20, KJV, says so.

> For what glory is it, if, when ye be buffeted for your faults, ye shall take it patiently? but if, when ye do well, and suffer for it, ye take it patiently, this is acceptable with God.

James speaks of the perseverance of the prophets. "Brothers, as an example of patience in the face of suffering, take the prophets who spoke in the name of the Lord" (5:10). The most prominent of these were Isaiah and Jeremiah.

For over sixty years, Isaiah proclaimed God's message to Judah and saw only superficial response. In fact, the nation backslid into idolatry. But, to the end of his days he pleaded for a return to the Lord, while he reassured the people of the Messiah's imminent coming and the establishment of his new and glorious kingdom.

Talking about getting beat up, Jeremiah suffered intense and continuous persecution, rejection, and imprisonment. Once he sank shoulder high in mud at the bottom of a pit. But he persevered. His days on earth ended when he was ministering to a remnant of poor Jewish immigrants in Egypt.

But our supreme example of patience is Jesus. After Israel rejected his claims, overlooked his healing ministry, spurned him personally, and even planned to kill him, he wept with deep compassion over their plight. Then unflinchingly, he offered himself as their Messiah.

And though his disciples misunderstood his lessons, showed little faith, and viewed much of what he said in terms of their personal gain, Christ patiently nurtured them. He knew that Pentecost was coming.[4]

Perseverance always seems to suggest the running of a race, the kind that millions observe every four years in the Olympics. Hebrews 12 acknowledges a roll call of persevering saints: the patriarchs, the prophets, the Lord. But then the spotlight turns on us. We, too, can possess enduring patience. "Therefore, since we are surrounded by such a great cloud of witnesses, let us throw off everything that hinders and the sin that so easily entangles, and let us run with perseverance the race marked out for us" (v. 1).

---

4. In presenting himself as their Messiah, Jesus accepted the lowliness that Zechariah had said would mark Israel's promised king (Zech. 9:9).

Most remarkable was our Lord's relationship with Judas at the last supper. He took bread, dipped it in meat juice, and offered it to the errant disciple. This identified him as the betrayer (John 13:21, 26). But, it did much more; "it demonstrated the ultimate in gracious patience." Jesus gave Judas the "morsel of honor, designating a highly esteemed guest." It was the "climatic appeal of His heart, beckoning the betrayer to turn from treachery to faith." Marchant, op. cit., pp. 23–24.

Second, in addition to perseverance, we must have the kind of patience that helps us to persist.

Receiving persecution with a Christian attitude is important, but no more crucial than hanging in there until our tasks are completed. Perseverance seems to imply an endurance against extreme trial. Persistence, on the other hand, suggests a bulldozer-type tenacity that helps us to carry out God's assignment.

My mind gravitates to the Japanese army officer who was stranded on an island after the war. Although he knew that the war was over and that his side had lost, he faithfully held out. Never would he be disloyal to his great emperor. He had received a sacred trust and would never go back on his word. Well, after decades they finally located the fellow and talked him into surrendering his sword. He returned to Tokyo as a hero, and as an amazing example of persistence.

Colossians instructs us to have this kind of devotion to God's agenda:

> And we pray . . . that you may live a life worthy of the Lord and may please him in every way: bearing fruit in every good work, growing in the knowledge of God, being strengthened with all power according to his glorious might so that you may have great . . . patience (1:10–11).

James tells us that our persistent patience should resemble that of a farmer who waits for his crops to grow. The harvest we anticipate is the glorious coming of our Lord (5:7–8). Until that day we are to drive forward with diligence.

Perseverance and persistence are two sides of the coin of patience that are extremely needed in our day of multiple pressures.

This was illustrated recently in the life of my friend Andy. He is far from lethargic and phlegmatic. Neither is he plagued with indolence or indifference. Andy is a go-getter—enthusiastic, energetic, exciting to be around. He demands much of himself.

Andy and his daughter Kari were stranded in Reno Airport. It was a hot summer afternoon. En route from Salem their plane had developed mechanical difficulties. Unfortunately, no other vehicles were available to land them at their Los Angeles destination.

The tempers of the other passengers were flaring. They screamed at the airlines personnel with vehemence. Their words were cutting and extremely insulting. Having to spend an unplanned night in Reno was considered the height of CAUP (cruel and unusual punishment).

How about Andy and Kari? Well, to be honest, they experienced many of the same emotions. Andy was scheduled to preach at our church the next morning.

But in the midst of this madhouse of confusion, the still, small voice whispered calmness to his heart. The one who said, "Peace be still" to the angry waves long ago, spoke the same words to my friend. And that peace saturated his inner spirit.

He immediately began to speak to his twelve-year-old daughter. "Kari, this is our opportunity to show these people that Christians are different. We're not going to react the way they are. Jesus is going to help us to stay calm." His daughter smiled and gave an affirming nod.

Guess what? Andy and Kari did make the flight home that night. Here is what occurred. After the noise subsided, my minister friend slipped up to the ticket counter and said to the employee, "Ma'am, I appreciate what you've had to go through. It hasn't been easy. I understand completely."

The lady looked very shocked. With trembling lips she replied, "You mean that you're not here to complain like the others?" He assured her that he was not, although he would like to get home to fulfill his preaching assignment.

She immediately went to work. His patience simply must be rewarded. She located another airlines flight that was leaving that evening. He and his daughter were offered two of the twelve seats that were left.

They had persevered and persisted patiently. And answering their prayer, our Lord chose to reward them. He often does that for his disciples who manifest his fruit. As James puts it, the "trying of [their] faith [worked] patience" (1:3, KJV). May we manifest this kind of patience when we encounter a similar situation of stress.

But, in addition to being patient, we must exhibit the fruit of kindness.

Passing Out the Milk

Of all the fruit of the Spirit, kindness is among those that is most universally understood. The "milk of human kindness" is quickly recognized and widely admired.

Perhaps that is why the Golden Rule exists in varying forms among the major religions of the world.[5] Doing unto others as we wish to be done unto is basic and appreciated wherever it occurs.

5. Throughout the centuries, people of all faiths have acknowledged the Golden Rule as a vital, intrinsic part of their faith. They have expressed it in the following ways.

Bahaiism: "If thou lookest toward justice, choose then for others what thou choosest for thyself. Blessed is he who prefers his brother before himself."

Brahmanism: "This is the sum of duty: Do naught unto others which would cause you pain if done to you."

Buddhism: "In five ways should a clansman minister to his friends and familiars: by generosity, courtesy and benevolence, treating them as he treats himself and by being as good as his word."

Christianity: "All things whatsoever you would that men should do to you, do you even to them, for this is the law and prophets."

Confucianism: "Is there one word which may serve as a rule to practice for all one's life? The master said, 'Is not reciprocity (sympathy, consideration) such a word? What you do not want done to yourself, do not unto others.'"

Hinduism: "The lifegiving breaths of other creatures are as dear to them as the breaths of one's own self. Men gifted with intelligence and purified souls should always treat others as they themselves wish to be treated."

Jainism: "Indifferent to worldly objects, a man should wander about, treating all creatures in the world as he himself would be treated."

Judaism: "Thou shalt love thy neighbor as thyself."

Mohammedanism: "No one of you is a believer until he loves for his brother what he loves for himself."

Sikhism: "As thou deemest thyself, do seem others; then shalt thou become a partner in heaven."

Shintoism: "Irrespective of their nationality, language, manners and culture, men should give mutual aid, and enjoy reciprocal, peaceful pleasure by showing in their conduct that they are brethren."

Likewise, we're quick to pick up on its opposite, unkindness.

Not long ago, Cherry and I visited a friend. Only a handful of families live in her condominium complex. Among them is at least one Christian. I know this, because he attends the same church as my friend. His father, greatly respected by my father, was one of the highest executives in our denomination.

On this particular visit, I chose to park behind my friend's garage. Inadvertently, I failed to pull the car in as far as I should have. Nevertheless, I was certainly not prepared for this curt note on my windshield upon my return:

> **Please** *do not* park like this.
> It took me 15 minutes, and one
> bump of the garage to get out.

Ironically, on the back side of the note was engraved lettering that referred to his church!

Now, I'm certainly not defending how I parked. Nor am I happy about the difficulty he encountered. My focus is on his response. Inherent in his words seemed to be a spirit of unkindness. Of resentment.

How easy it is for us to react in a knee-jerk, unkind fashion when we've been inconvenienced!

But, again, how greatly appreciated is the kindness that we bestow. One of the nicest statements that is ever made at a funeral is, "He was a kind man," or, "She was a kind lady." In the final essence, that means more to people than how much wealth we accumulate, how many degrees we earn, or how many lofty positions we hold. Kindness is highly valued.

Taoism: "Regard your neighbor's gain as your own gain, and regard your neighbor's loss as your own loss."

Zoroastrianism: "That nature alone is good which refrains from doing unto another whatsoever is not good for itself."

The biblical word for kindness if *chrestotes*, meaning "a gentle or tender action, a spirit of compassion and concern."[6] It reflects a nonoffensive disposition that causes us to go out of our way to help and encourage.

Kindness is an attribute that is rooted in the very fiber of God's character.

> And God raised us up with Christ and seated us with him in the heavenly realms in Christ Jesus, in order that in the coming ages he might show the incomparable riches of his grace, expressed in his kindness to us in Christ Jesus (Eph. 2:6–7).

Kindness also is synonymous with the grace of Jesus, whereby we have eternal salvation. Titus says so.

> But when the kindness and love of God our Savior appeared, he saved us, not because of righteous things we had done, but because of his mercy (3:4–5a).

But, kindness is even more than a godly attribute, and more than a fruit of the Spirit. It is a command.

> Therefore, as God's chosen people, holy and dearly loved, clothe yourselves with compassion, kindness, humility, gentleness and patience (Col. 3:12).

It is important to realize that this fruit is usually evidenced in behind-the-scenes service. Kindness

offers a cup of cold water in the name of Christ (Matt. 10:42).

visits widows and orphans in their distress (James 1:27).

stops to help the injured traveler on the road (Luke 10:29–37).

considers others as more important than ourselves (Phil. 2:3–4).

6. John Moore, "Kindness," *Moody Monthly*, op. cit., pp. 24–25.

Much in our culture mitigates kindness. Books instruct us to be on guard to protect ourselves. It's a jungle out there, every person for himself, and we're foolish to put ourselves out for another.

So, rather than seeking ways to exhibit this fruit, we're intent on maximizing our own interests. We knife into parking spaces that others are waiting on, take cuts in lines, refrain from telling salesclerks that they have mistakenly charged us too little. In short, we're out for number one, and some of us haven't even assigned numbers to others.

Sure, we warm up around Christmas or special occasions. By turning up our kindness mechanism full blast during such times, we assuage our consciences concerning the rest of the year.

Also, we're kind to persons whom, we perceive can do us good. This is called "pump-priming." Or ones who are especially kind to us. This is termed "back-scratching."

But, as Christ's redeemed and Spirit-filled followers, we must offer our milk of kindness to others. People who seem cold and unreceptive. People who are too proud (or ashamed) to ask for help. People who don't deserve our overtures—in short, people who were like us before our kind Lord reached down to us to make all things new.

Of course, it costs to be kind. Inconvenience. Overwork. Monetary sacrifice. The list goes on. And we can think of a million reasons to detour this task. As Phillip Keller states,

> Kindness is more than running a bluff on beleaguered people. It is more than pretending to be concerned by their condition. True kindness goes beyond the play acting of simulated sighs and crocodile tears. It is getting involved with the personal sorrows and strains of other lives to the point where it may well cost me pain—real pain—and some inconvenience.[7]

7. W. Phillip Keller, *A Gardener Looks at the Fruits of the Spirit* (Waco, TX: Word Books, 1979), pp. 126–127.

But, when we consider how Christ inconvenienced himself for us, our cost seems minimal. Even nonexistent.

We must be kind out of gratitude for his kindness to us, out of respect for other people, the apex of his creation. And even more than these reasons, our kindness will be generated from a heart saturated with his Holy Spirit.

Keller illustrates kindness by referring to the well-known missionary of yesteryear, David Livingstone.

His foot safaris took him thousands of miles through uncharted lands and among strange and savage tribes. Yet, wherever his footprints were left behind, there "remained the legacy of the love of Christ expressed in his simple, humble kindness to the natives." Long after his earthly journey was finished, he was remembered in Africa as the kind doctor. "What greater accolade could any man earn?"[8]

Having spoken of kindness, we now turn our attention to a fruit of the Spirit that is closely related. Let's explore the rich dimensions of goodness.

"If I've Told You Once,
I've Told You a Thousand Times!"

Whenever our mothers say this oft-repeated line, invariably they want us to be good.

The French mother typically says to her child, "Be wise!" The German mother commands. "Do your duty!" And the Wintu Indian mother declares, "Obey the tribal rules."

But, the American mother's usual admonition is, "Be good!" Like little Jack Horner, of nursery rhyme fame, she wants her son to legitimately declare, "Oh, what a good boy am I."

Not only do mothers value goodness, it is considered

8. Ibid., p. 133.

a prized commodity throughout society. We usually attribute it to things. My wife's cherry cheesecake is "Uuuummm good!" Also, we attach it to activities. When our sports hero makes the winning shot, home run, or touchdown, we often say, "Good going!"

Usually, what isn't good is considered bad or, at best, mediocre. And most of us strive for the good.[9] By this, we mostly mean what seems right, comfortable, or ideal, based on the emotional and mental judgments that we (or those we respect) make.[10]

That's our broad and ambiguous connotation of the term good or goodness. How does the Bible define this important concept?

Paul uses his Greek word *agathosune*, which is defined as "virtue equipped at every point."[11] Uprightness and generosity are implied.

How does this word differ from kindness (*chrestos*)? Let's chart the two essential contrasts.

Kindness (*chrestos*)	Goodness (*agathosune*)
inward disposition of the heart	habitual actions in which the inward disposition reveals itself[12]
restricted to a focus on helping	includes helping, but also rebuking, correcting, and disciplining[13]

9. On the other hand, there is a substantial element in our society that attempts to depreciate moral goodness. Those so identified are commonly termed "dogooders," "goody-goodies" or "goody-two-shoes." Such jargon implies that moral goodness is synonymous with being weak, insipid, and even laughable. Ibid., p. 140.

10. Webster's *New World Dictionary* lists seventeen categories of definitions for "good." And each one has three or four meanings.

11. The Greek root word for "good" (*agathos*) appears 102 times in the New Testament, and fills two columns in Arndt and Gingrich's *Greek/English Lexicon of the New Testament*. The definitions include such words as genuine, uncontaminated, honorable, healthy, generous, desirable, pleasant, dependable, honest, loyal.

12. Alexander Maclaren, *Expositions of Holy Scripture: Second Corinthians, Galatians and Philippians* (New York: Hodder and Stoughton, no date), p. 165.

13. William Barclay, op. cit., p. 56.

We enjoy singing the chorus "God Is So Good." And we couldn't be more theologically on target. Our heavenly Father is the very essence of goodness.[14]

When Moses asked to see God's glory, he responded, "I Myself will make all My goodness pass before you . . . and I will be gracious to whom I will be gracious, and will show compassion on whom I will show compassion" (Exod. 33:19, NASB).

Following the dedication of the newly completed Temple, the Israelites "went to their tents joyful and glad of heart for all the goodness that the LORD had shown to David His servant and to Israel His people" (1 Kings 8:66, NASB; cf. Neh. 9:25, 35).

The psalmists declared God's goodness in providing for physical and spiritual needs. "Do not remember the sins of my youth or my transgressions; according to Thy loving kindness remember Thou me, for Thy goodness' sake, O LORD" (25:7, NASB). "I would have despaired unless I had believed that I would see the goodness of the LORD in the land of the living" (27:13, NASB; cf. 68:10; 107:9). Also, they spoke of God's goodness in protection. "How great is Thy goodness, which Thou has stored up for those who fear Thee, which Thou has wrought for those who take refuge in Thee, before the sons of men" (31:19, NASB).

And in the triumphant climax of most everyone's favorite Psalm, David declares, "Surely goodness and mercy shall follow me all the days of my life: and I will dwell in the house of the LORD for ever" (23:6, KJV).

14. In the original Anglo-Saxon, the very word *good* carried the same connotation as "God." God was considered good, and good was regarded as belonging essentially to God. The goodness of God isn't some "soft, spineless, sentimental indulgence of sensuality," as W. Phillip Keller declares: "Not some passing mood of the moment that makes one feel so good. It is not an emotional high in which reality fades away into some rosy glow of mystical magic.

"[His] goodness is the rugged reality of [His] coming to grips with the awfulness of sin . . . that invincible power . . . overcoming evil . . . the greatness of His love that dispels our despair and brings life out of our death . . . His generosity and graciousness in giving us Himself by His own Gracious Spirit. It is the enormous energy of His light and life extinguishing the evil in and around [us]. This goodness is the pulsating, powerful performance of right in the midst of wrong all around us." W. Phillip Keller, op. cit., pp. 141–42.

Because God is "the Source and Giver of every good and perfect gift" (James 1:17) we have an abiding hope. Why? His goodness translates into grace through his Son, whereby we might have fulfilling life on earth (John 10:10) and eternal life in heaven.

W. Phillip Keller, in his book entitled *A Gardener Looks at the Fruits of the Spirit*, offers this insight:

> Because God is good we have hope. Like the prodigal son back from the pigsty, there is a gold ring for our soil-stained hand—a white robe to clothe our sweatstained body—fresh sandals for our dung-stained feet—kisses for our tear-stained cheeks.[15]

As his goodness is bridged to our lives by Jesus, we will be certain to manifest it. Second Corinthians 5:23 (Phillips) says, "For God caused Christ . . . to be sin for our sakes, so that in Christ we might be made good with the goodness of God."

Therefore, we will first of all be good. To the very core of our being, goodness will prevail. And the result is a deep, abiding peace that this world can never know.

As Christians, we know that the truly great person is a good person, and the really good person is always great. He has lofty ideals, strong character, noble purposes, reliable conduct, trustworthy integrity.[16]

But, when we are good with God's goodness, we can expect some discomforts to occur. How do we know? Because they happened to our Lord during his earthly sojourn. Others will polarize in reacting to us. Either we'll strongly attract them, or they'll be decidedly repelled by our presence. Since fewer will be attracted to us, because most are traveling in the opposite direction of goodness, we're likely to feel pretty isolated and lonely.

Without a doubt these two realities are true concerning

15. Ibid., p. 143.
16. Ibid., p. 142.

the secular world. But, unfortunately, they can stalk us in the church. Even in that environment, persons fail to relentlessly pursue God's goodness—which puts them at odds with good people. Paul puts it plainly. "For what fellowship hath righteousness with unrighteousness? and what communion hath light with darkness?" (2 Cor. 6:14b, KJV).

Nevertheless, in being good we have nothing to fear, hide or protect. Nor do we have any need to apologize. God's goodness makes us simple, open, and uncomplicated persons who live with open hearts and hands. He supplies our every need. And as for our loneliness, he becomes our intimate friend. As the writer of Proverbs declares, "There is a friend who sticks closer than a brother" (18:24b).

But, in addition to being good we will also do good. We will sacrificially share what we are and have. This will include generosity with our time, talents, interests, strengths, energies, and capacities.

What we own we gladly place in Christ's hands. And like the loaves and fishes of old, it is blessed and multiplied a thousand times to enrich others' lives.

In a very real sense, we must think of ourselves as only the middlemen, giving to others what God has given to us. Colossians speaks of "bearing fruit in every good work" (1:10). Titus says, "Our people must learn to devote themselves to doing what is good" (3:14). Here's one of my favorites, Galatians 6:10: "Therefore, as we have opportunity, let us do good to all people, especially to those who belong to the family of believers."

The word used for goodness is translated "generous" in the story of the rich landowner (Matt. 20:1–15). His goodness is expressed in a generous act that did not rest on the recipient's performance. The latter did not deserve payment. Rather, the landowner gave because he desired the worker's well-being, just as Jesus does for us.

Likewise, we must generously give without considering the issue of fairness or deservability of those we give to. Granted. Saturated with our free enterprise mentality, such generosity is difficult for us. We say things such as, "Let them earn it like I had to do." "I'm not about to perpetuate their laziness by giving them a handout." "They've got their problems, I've got mine."

Nevertheless, we must continuously consider how undeserving we are, and how our good Lord and Savior gave to us with a generosity unparalleled. The very least we can do is return the favor to his needy children.

He expects all of us who claim to have his goodness in our hearts to

help the downtrodden	bring "oil of joy" to those
bind up broken hearts	who mourn
set prisoners free	spread light and cheer where
lift the fallen	there is darkness
feed the hungry	share the good news of God's
comfort the confused	gracious love to the lost[17]

Now, of course, being and doing good in the biblical sense is light years away from doing good works to gain merit. The first is a natural response to the indwelling Holy Spirit; the second is based on the selfish desire to be seen and praised.

Question: How can we become good persons and start growing in that goodness? Again, W. Phillip Keller makes four excellent practical suggestions.

1. Contemplate the cross. Prayerfully read the accounts of the crucifixion. Meditate over the tremendous cost to God, to Christ—who was made sin so that we might be good with his goodness. Accept his offer. Thank him. Allow him to implant goodness in the stony soil of your heart.

2. Ask Jesus to totally invade the territory of your life. Having asked him to establish a beachhead, now

17. Ibid., p. 146.

invite him to occupy. Give him liberty to love and
change you, so that you become readied to exude his
goodness to others.

3. As he lives in you, and you in him, keep the ground
of your life clear, clean, and uncluttered. Be repen-
tant of sins and penitent of unintentional faults,
with genuine sorrow. Obey promptly, joyfully, simply (cf. Phil. 2:12–15).

4. Remind yourself always that you are the recipient,
not the originator of every gift, possession and attribute that you own. All come from Jesus. Be deeply
grateful for his inestimable generosity.[18]

A simple, four-step prescription for his goodness
within—as well as without. We're well advised to follow
it closely.

Patience. Kindness. Goodness. Christian qualities of
character that we all need. Qualities that will serve us
well as we relate to other people. Particularly those with
whom we interface in close proximity.

These qualities can extract tension, lessen stress, provide a new, upbeat perspective that will make our worlds
better. They are fruit that we in the Christian community
need to produce and reveal.

But one more cluster of spiritual fruit remains. They
likewise greatly help us in our relationships with others.
Let's see how.

18. Ibid., pp. 148–149.

Not every slight requires a rejoinder; every fool need not be reminded that he is one.—Buckminster Fuller

God breaks up the private life of His saints, and makes it into a thorofare for the world—and for Himself.
—Oswald Chambers

Here am I, Lord; send my brother.—Prayer overheard

11

Fruit Cluster #3: Faithfulness, Gentleness, Self-control

One more cluster of Son-ripened fruit remains. This one includes three other important varieties that we must transport: faithfulness, gentleness, and self-control.

They help us relate with and respond to society in general. The system that confronts us daily. The secular culture that impinges upon us with never ceasing pressure. The Satan-dominated world that continually tempts us to dump the fruit that the Holy Spirit has given us.[1]

1. Watchman Nee, in his thought-provoking book *Love Not the World*, discusses Satan's control of the world order. He terms it "the mind behind the system." The prince of our world (Satan) governs an ordered system of unseen powers which have one main purpose: to deceive those who seek to follow God, who is the Spirit of truth. Satan seeks to enmesh men in his system. In Nee's words: "Salvation is not so much a personal question of sins forgiven or hell avoided (although it is that): (but, in addition) . . . it is a system from which we come out. When I am saved, I make my exodus out of one whole world and my entry into another. I am saved now out of that whole organized realm which Satan has constructed in defiance of the purpose of God." Watchman Nee, *Love Not the World* (Wheaton, IL: Tyndale, 1968), p. 38.

Alexander Maclaren puts it succinctly. "[These three fruit]. . . point to the world in which the Christian life is to be lived, a scene of difficulties and oppositions."[2] To employ the well-known phrase of J.B. Phillips, this triad keeps our alien world from "squeezing us into its mold."[3]

We can think of them in many ways, as protective clauses in our spiritual insurance policy, or shock absorbers that cushion us from society's bumpy roads. But, there is another image that really explains their extreme value more than any other.

Sometime ago I visited a marine life park. There were playful porpoises and dolphins, intelligent whales and sea lions, and many other captivating specimens of sea life. All the displays and performances were interesting.

I must say, however, that none compared to the deep sea diver's time of hand-feeding the fish. As we gazed into the glass tank from a lower lever, I saw all species of fish rapidly swim to her. Some were so small that they could hardly be seen. Others were gigantic. Most looked colorful and tame. But, then there were the sharks that looked very threatening.

The diver must have fed them for over an hour, then she glided to the surface.

Suddenly, an inspiring thought struck me. This lady had entered an alien environment. Without her oxygen tank, she would not have survived more than three minutes. If she had drunk ocean water, even in a small quantity, she would have perished.

Yet, our fish-feeding friend survived. Not only that, she seemed to thoroughly enjoy her task. Why was life so comfortable down there? Because her life-giving oxygen was supplied from an external source. She wasn't forced to rely on her immediate environment.

In a very real sense, this world is an alien environment

2. Alexander Maclaren, *Expositions of Holy Scripture: Second Corinthians, Galatians and Philippians* (New York: Hodder and Stoughton, no date), p. 166.
3. Romans 12:2

for us. No wonder we sing, "This world is not my home, I'm just a' travelin' through. My treasure is laid up somewhere beyond the blue."

Nevertheless, we're able to survive. More than that, we're able to enjoy life to its fullest—cultivating loving relationships, manifesting patience, exuding kindness and goodness—because of one reason: Jesus supplies us with a spiritual oxygen supply. As a result, he creates for us a new internal environment, and we can become "more than conquerors through him who loved us" (Rom. 8:37).

Bring out the microscope. We're about to take a scrutinizing look at the fruit of faithfulness. Unlocking its valuable secrets can add a remarkable dimension to our lives.

If It's Broke, Don't Fix It!

Most of us have heard the oft-repeated adage, "If it ain't broke, don't fix it!" Fully aware of my mechanical limitations, my wife tells me, "Even if it's broke, don't attempt to fix it. Call the repairman." Past attempts on my part have resulted in emotional and financial disaster.

Unfortunately for all of us, things continually break. Garbage disposals freeze. Cars won't start. Locks jam. Water heaters give out. In spite of our technological advancements, our gadgets and toys are unreliable.

Also, people are unreliable. A famous long-distance runner, in commenting on American athletes, said, "They're sensational in spirit, but get fagged out in the stretch."[4] Likewise, employers ulcerate because of absenteeism and tardiness. Christian education directors in churches cringe when the telephone rings on Sunday morning. Usually it's someone bailing out of a responsibility. As one said recently, "It's amazing what a sore hangnail can do to the Kingdom of God!"

4. Voiced by track star Herb Elliot.

Our world values reliability, trustworthiness, and fidelity. To be consistent is to be admired and appreciated. To be a flake is to be resented.

To paraphrase a quote I recently saw, nothing in the world will take the place of faithfulness.

Talent will not. Nothing is more common than unsuccessful people with talent.

Genius will not. Unrewarded genius is almost a proverb.

Education will not. The world is full of educated derelicts.

Faithfulness and determination alone will![5]

I couldn't help but laugh. In a recent major league allstar game, one player proved to be completely unreliable. Here was a fellow who had been selected by the fans. A coveted honor. Yet, he somehow couldn't bring himself to get ready for the big game.

Amazing! There he was on camera before tens of millions of television viewers wearing a ragtag outfit. It began when he forgot—yes *forgot*—to bring his uniform. Still desiring to play, he went to work putting together a makeshift arrangement. He bought a shirt from a replica shop. Wrote his number on the back with a felt-tip marker. Borrowed socks from a player on another team. And purchased his cap at the airport. What a sight!

We laugh, but how many of those we know are content to just get by? To expend the absolute minimum amount of effort? To refuse to be motivated except by crisis?

Faithfulness is a highly prized spiritual fruit. It means getting our act together. Having a self-starter that works. Making it known that people can count on us. We won't let them down. We won't flake out in the stretch.

5. Larry Richards and Norm Wakefield, *Fruit of the Spirit* (Grand Rapids, MI: Zondervan Publishing House, 1981), p. 108.

The Greek word for faithfulness, *pistos*, is translated many ways throughout Scripture: reliability, good faith, dependability, loyalty, assurance, and trustworthiness.

A recent Dennis the Menace cartoon has the little character holding up a handful of flowers to Mr. Wilson, and asking, "How can anything so pretty and clean come out of dirt?"[6]

We can legitimately ask the same question about ourselves as Christians. Galatians chapter five describes all the ugliness of the flesh. People so enslaved are doing little more than groveling in sin's dirt.

Yet, because of God's faithfulness, we are transformed into a bouquet of Christian graces. The point is this: Because of our heavenly Father's gift of faithfulness to us, we can exude faithfulness. In Paul's words, this can make us "a fragrant offering. . . pleasing to God" (Phil. 4:18).

Indeed, our God is faithful. 1 Thessalonians 5:24 declares, "The one who calls you is faithful." God is trustworthy. Available. Dependable. Never too busy, distracted, or tired. That's why, with assurance, we sing,

> Great is Thy faithfulness, O God my Father.
> There is no shadow of turning with Thee;
> Thou changest not, Thy compassions they fail not;
> As Thou hast been Thou forever wilt be. . .
> Great is Thy faithfulness, Lord, unto me![7]

What God says, he means. What he promises, he fulfills. What he offers, he gives. It's his nature to come through in the pinch, in the nick of time. He is totally faithful.

Likewise, Jesus our Lord is faithful. In fact, "Faithful" is one of his names (cf. Rev. 19:11). The term also describes

---

6. Donald Baker, "Faithfulness," *Moody Monthly*, September, 1983, p. 26.

7. *Worship in Song Hymnal* (Kansas City, MO: Lillenas Publishing Company, 1972), p. 86.

his witness (cf. Rev. 1:5) and his priesthood (cf. Heb. 2:17). We can fully depend on him to bring us into the presence of God.

He does more than commit; he covenants with us. Commitments are made and broken, depending on changes in circumstances. Covenants remain eternally. His are as good as his Word. And we can't imagine anything more reliable than that!

With this in mind, it is obvious that he expects us who have received the fruit of his Spirit to manifest faithfulness. This in spite of our perpetual propensity toward fickleness and flakiness.

One Corinthians 4:1–2 spells this out. "So then, men ought to regard us as servants of Christ and as those entrusted with the secret things of God. Now it is required that those who have been given a trust must prove faithful."

In his own parable of the talents, our Lord exalted the servant who demonstrated dependability. "His master replied, 'Well done, good and faithful servant! You have been faithful with a few things; I will put you in charge of many things. Come and share your master's happiness!'" (Matt. 25:21).

The emphasis here is on being diligent in the small and seemingly insignificant tasks. They are but precursors to momentous assignments, and gateways to our eternal reward.

Could this mean eventual martyrdom? Yes. That has certainly occurred in the lives of believers throughout the centuries—and even today it happens frequently. But the Christian martyr is triumphant. As Walt Emerson said,

> The martyr cannot be dishonored. Every lash inflicted is a tongue of fame; every prison a more illustrious abode; every burned book or house enlightens the world; every suppressed word reverberates through the earth from side to side.[8]

8. Walt Emerson, source unknown.

Church father Tertullian spoke the truth when he said, "The blood of the martyr is the seed of the church." Those faithful ones who have paid this supreme price are our heroes.[9] The very thought of what they went through should inspire our hearts.

Nevertheless, the likelihood is that we'll never be martyrs. Our faithfulness will be shown in other, less dramatic, manners. Things like completing assignments, keeping promises, paying bills, keeping appointments, doing work on time, honoring commitments, maintaining priorities—God's priorities.

When his Spirit within causes these to occur, we transcend the making of resolutions, which we're habitually doing at New Years. Rather, we'll experience inner revolution (2 Cor. 5:17). The latter, in contrast to the former, is generated from the core of our being.

Unlike so many today, let's vow to not sputter out in the stretch. Drawing upon God's power, let's remain faithful to the end. After all, we aren't hanging in there alone. In the very last verse of Matthew's Gospel, Jesus encourages us with these words: "And surely I am with you always, to the very end of the age" (Matt. 28:20).

Faithfulness is important. But so is the next fruit that we will now turn to, namely gentleness.

Speak Softly, and Carry No Stick!

Theodore Roosevelt (1858–1919) was our twenty-sixth President. Historians tell us that he was a feisty character, whose slogan was, "Speak softly, and carry a big stick." The idea was this: Don't threaten with words; strike at the enemy with promptness and might. To underscore his

9. "Be of good comfort," said Latimer to Ridley as they died at the stake together—at the time of Queen Mary in the 1500s. "We shall this day light a candle by God's grace, in England, and it shall never be put out."

Chrysostom advised Christians to give the name of a saint to their children, then to tell them constantly about the saint's life throughout their childhood. Hopefully, they would then grow up to model the saint's behavior.

belief in this philosophy, he sent America's "white fleet" around the world. The message went out loud and clear: "Don't mess with the U.S.A., or you'll be sorry!"

Stick theology is *not* biblical theology, regardless of what some super-patriots would have us believe. Our Lord carried a simple staff, not a threatening club.

Truly gentle persons are as rare as southern California snowstorms. Most of us react with a vengeance when experiencing the slightest provocation.

The other day, however, I found an exception to this rule. Here's a fellow who may have had a legitimate right to be less gentle than he was. I'll allow him to relate his unbelievable account, which is contained in this letter to his supervisor.

When I arrived at the construction site I found that a hurricane had knocked some bricks off the top of the building. So, I rigged up a beam, with a pulley on the highest level. Then, I hoisted up a couple barrels full of bricks. After fixing the damaged area at the top, I noticed that a lot of bricks were left over. So, I went down to the bottom and began releasing the line. That's when the problems began.

Unfortunately, the barrel of bricks was heavier that I was—and before I realized what was happening, the barrel started coming down—jerking me up. I decided to hang on, since I was now too far off the ground to let go. Halfway up, I met the barrel of bricks coming down fast. I received a hard blow on my shoulder. Then, I continued to the top—banging my head against the beam, and finding my fingers jammed in the pulley.

When the barrel hit the ground hard, it burst its bottom, spilling out the bricks. Well, I was now heavier than the barrel, so I started going down again. With high speed, halfway down, I met the barrel coming up fast—and received severe injuries to my shins. When I landed on the ground, I hit the pile of bricks—getting several deep and painful bruises.

At this point, I must have lost presence of mind, because I let go of the grip of the line, and the barrel came down fast—giving me another blow on my shoulder and head. And putting me in the hospital.

I respectfully request sick leave.[10]

I surmise that most of us would have come out of that situation swinging, crying, threatening to sue, or all three! Ours would not have been a polite and gentle request for sick leave.

Why aren't we Americans more gentle? For one thing, we feel that being gentle makes us vulnerable. People may take advantage of us, mistake us for being a pawn. A chump. An easy mark.

For another, we who are macho-oriented males shy away from gentleness because it may make us appear wimpish. Real he-men, we feel, need to be aggressive and competitive. Gentleness is for women, children, and gentlemen.

Question: What does the term *gentle* mean when listed as one of the spiritual fruit?

The Greek word is *praotes*, which William Barclay says is the "most untranslatable of words." It has no less than three meanings in the New Testament

1. submissive to the will of God (cf. Matt. 5:5; 11:29; 21:5)

2. teachable in all good things—not too proud to learn (cf. James 1:21)

3. considerate toward our fellow humans (1 Cor. 4:21; 2 Cor. 10:1; Eph. 4:2)[11]

The third of these meanings is used most often.

---

10. Source unknown. Presented in a sermon.
11. William Barclay, *The Daily Study Bible: The Letters to the Galatians and Ephesians* (Philadelphia, PA: The Westminster Press, 1954), pp. 56–57.

Through the centuries, gentleness has referred to being tame—what a wild horse must become if he is to be of any use.

For the Christian, gentleness means being tamed by God's Holy Spirit. When we're gentle, we're tame toward others. In difficult circumstances. When others are inconsiderate. We're tender when others are abrasive, quiet when others are aloud and coarse.[12]

There's really nothing wimpish or cowardly about that. In fact, the opposite is true. When we are truly gentle, we demonstrate strength, God's strength.

For our Lord, gentleness was a life experience. It was his natural, spiritual reflex. Even while suffering on the cross, he was considerate of his mother's need for care and safety (cf. John 19:26–27).

In Matthew's Gospel, Jesus says,

> Take my yoke upon you and learn from me, for I am gentle
> and humble in heart, and you will find rest for your souls.
> For my yoke is easy and my burden is light" (11:29–30).

When approaching Jerusalem for the last time, Jesus chose to ride on a donkey. Why? To reveal his gentle spirit.

> This took place to fulfill what was spoken through the
> prophet: "Say to the Daughter of Zion, 'See, your king
> comes to you, gentle and riding on a donkey, on a colt, the
> foal of a donkey'" (Matt. 21:4–5; cf. Zech. 9:9).

In the nineteenth century, history records that Chancellor Bismarck of Prussia chose to make his grand entrance into Jerusalem on a white horse. And he was accompanied by such a large army of officials that a section of the wall had to be removed.

Not so with our Lord. He chose a donkey. Why? Unlike the ostentatious Chancellor, he was gentle of heart.

And if he was gentle and lowly—being the very Son of

12. Arthur Evans Gay, Jr., "Gentleness," *Moody Monthly*, September, 1983, p. 27.

God—we can assure ourselves that we're expected to be the same. Especially since he has provided this fruit through the blessed Holy Spirit. Like the lemons that hung on our backyard tree, his fruit of gentleness is ours for the plucking.

His Beatitudes declare, "Blessed are the poor in spirit. . . . Blessed are the meek" (Matt. 5:3, 5). Another way of saying the same truth is that we need to manifest gentleness and thereby reveal our humility.

When writing to the Colossians, Paul said, "Therefore, as God's chosen people, holy and dearly loved, clothe yourselves with compassion, kindness, humility, gentleness and patience" (3:12).

Any time we clothe ourselves with garments, they are displayed for everyone to see. We're making a fashion statement. We're wearing a costume that says something significant about who we are. Let's be certain to include gentleness in our wardrobe!

The disciple called Rock instructs us to be gentle when presenting the gospel to others—not harsh, condemning, insulting, not with a distasteful air of self-righteousness. Rather, we are to do so with gentleness.

> Always be prepared to give an answer to everyone who asks you to give the reason for the hope that you have. But do this with gentleness and respect (1 Peter 3:15b).

How about when we're being unfairly confronted, or when people come at us with slanderous remarks? When Timothy encountered such situations, Paul instructed him to

> [not] have anything to do with foolish and stupid arguments, because. . . they produce quarrels. And the Lord's servant must not quarrel; instead he must be kind to everyone, able to teach, not resentful. Those who oppose him he must gently instruct, in the hope that God will grant them repentance leading them to a knowledge of the truth (2 Tim. 2:23–25).

The point is crystal clear. We are to display and transport the fruit of gentleness.

In our *conversation*. Gentle words are comforting and edifying. They reflect a heart filled with God's presence.

In our *conduct*. Proverbs 16:7 tells us: "When a man's ways are pleasing to the *Lord*, he makes even his enemies live at peace with him." Concerning fellow Christians, Paul exhorts, "If someone is caught in a sin, you who are spiritual should restore him gently" (Gal. 6:1).

Finally, in our conflict. As Timothy was told above, quarreling gets us nowhere!

Norman Wakefield summarizes gentleness in this manner:

> When I am indwelt by the spirit of gentleness my own life is enriched. I enjoy more harmonious relationships with others. God's indwelling peace allows me to approach uncertain and stressful situations without anxiety.
>
> In the strength of meekness I can act with gentleness. I am able to be a better steward of my energy because I do not dissipate it with anxiety, strife or frustration.[13]

May gentleness reign in our hearts. In spite of this world's sea of beckoning fingers that lure us to react with abruptness and hostility.

We can become truly gentle. We can possess this Christlike strength.

There is one more fruit that God's Spirit produces in us. Like gentleness, self-control can provide enrichment and fulfillment in the midst of a morally bankrupt world. Let's examine it closely.

Leashes and Lashes

In describing the kind of restraint persons should exhibit, one writer appealed for willpower that is both a leash and a lash.

13. Richards and Wakefield, op. cit., pp. 120–121.

As any poodle in my neighborhood can tell you, a leash restricts his behavior. He isn't able to wander off.

A lash is used on a racehorse to make him change his behavior. Either he's made to go faster or to get back in his lane.

In essence, this is exactly how we should be able to control ourselves. *Leashing* or restricting ourselves from doing impulsive, self-defeating things. *Lashing* or motivating ourselves to excel, together with chiding ourselves when we fail.[14]

Self-control is a remarkable, greatly admired quality in our society. But the Chinese do more than admire this virtue, they put it into practice. Perhaps rooted in their eastern religion heritage, the orientals are adept at conditioning themselves to be passive, respectful, reserved.[15]

I had to smile recently when I came upon the rejection letter that was sent from a Chinese publisher to an aspiring author. Talk about polite ways to say no, this one takes the cake.

Dear respected sir:

We have read your manuscript with boundless delight. But if we were to publish your book, it would be impossible for us to publish work of lower standard. And as it is unthinkable that, in the next 3,000 years, we shall see its

14. Plato antedated Sigmund Freud's tripartite explanation of the self by declaring that every person has a horse named Passion, and another one called Reason. These two animals run hitched-up in the same team. Furthermore, they continually battle for supremacy. The charioteer is the core self that must unsparingly use the whip on these animals when either attempts to dominate the other. [Note: The horse Passion is roughly equated to Freud's id; Reason is a near approximation of the super ego; and the charioteer might be construed as the ego.]

15. Buddhism, Taoism and the other eastern religions emphasize the importance of being passive, of allowing reality to flow into us by noninvolvement and noneffort (wo-wei). The idea is to empty oneself of sensual concerns, through meditation and other means. Only then can "cosmic consciousness" (a vague, God-like, universal spirit) take over our beings. Whereas western religions accentuate doing, eastern ones emphasize being—or even nonbeing. [See Ernest Benz. "On Understanding Non-Christian Religions," in *Religion, Culture and Society: A Reader in the Sociology of Religion,* ed. Louis Schneider, (New York: John Wiley and Sons, Incorporated, 1964), pp. 3–9.]

equal, we are regretfully compelled to return your divine composition. We beg you a thousand times to overlook our short sight and timidity.

Your humble servants[16]

Now *that's* a controlled response, compared with the kind that I have received—the don't-call-us-we'll-call-you variety.

Whether related to how we communicate, act, or think, self-control is a great virtue. Rather than leading to rigidity, it more often results in freedom. Just as the tightness of the violin string allows the musician to freely engender beautiful sounds, so the control we exercise gives us latitude to experience more of life. Persons who can concentrate come up with creative ideas. Individuals who can focus attention on their jobs—be they in offices or on athletic fields—are freed to excel!

When we lack self-control, we invariably feel the need to fake, fudge (misrepresent facts and figures), or finagle by making excuses.

On her syndicated radio program, Psychologist Dr. Joyce Brothers states that we customarily make three kinds of excuses to cover our ineptitude.

1. not me ("This is a clear case of mistaken identity. I'm not the culprit!")

2. not so bad ("Sure, I'm guilty, but the results aren't nearly as tragic as you think!")

3. not all the picture ("You bet, I did it, and the effects are pretty devastating. But, there are mitigating circumstances that should make you excuse my behavior.")[17]

Here's the irony of lacking self-control: It often requires

16. Source unknown. Read at a conference on leadership.
17. Joyce Brothers, heard on KABC radio in Los Angeles, July 29, 1987.

more time, money, and energy to cover up the shabby results of our incompetence than does simple TCB (taking care of business).

This principle may figure into why Paul includes self-control in his list of spiritual fruit. The Greek word is *egkrateia*, which implies "the kind of self-mastery that makes us into true servants." According to William Barclay, the term was used to describe an emperor who never allowed his private interests to influence his role in government. He had the willpower to separate the two.

Paul employed the word to describe an athlete's discipline of his body. "And every man that striveth for the mastery is temperate in all things. Now they *do it* to obtain a corruptible crown; but we an incorruptible" (1 Cor. 9:25, KJV).

In the same Letter, he relates self-control to sexual temptations. "But if they [unmarried and widows] cannot control themselves, they should marry, for it is better to marry than to burn with passion" (7:9).

Peter instructs us to "make every effort to add to [our] faith...self-control" (2 Peter 1:5, 6). It's in his list of essentials—and it must be in ours.

And as Norman Wakefield states, life for many of us is much like an ocean. "The mire of failure is constantly being stirred up. Instability controls [us] like unseen currents. Crashing waves break up the little order [we] have. For [us] the hope of self-control [seems like] a vanishing dream."[18]

But, when the love of Jesus floods into our hearts and saturates us completely, when God's Spirit reigns supreme, then self-control will be the natural expression of our lives. It will somehow fit with what we are and what we aspire to be. This is in contrast to the bite-the-bullet, radical denial kind of self-control that the world speaks about.

18. Richards and Wakefield, op. cit., p. 132.

This contrast is vividly revealed in a story I recently heard. A Christian lady was married to an ogre. A cruel taskmaster who was impossible to please. When she served him perfectly, he ignored mentioning it. When she failed concerning some minute task, she was quick to hear his fear-inducing roar.

Her husband went so far as to make a long list of his demands. They filled an entire page with small print. Just glancing at it gave her a headache and depression.

Well, in the providence of God, the man suddenly died. She was released from her torturous imprisonment.

After a few years she met a truly Christian gentleman—the polar opposite of her previous husband. They fell in love and married, and their love continued to accelerate for one another because of their oneness in Christ.

One particular day she found herself cleaning the house. She opened a drawer, looked down, and froze. There it was. *That* note. That list of cruel, impossible demands. How could he have possibly expected so much?

Then something very enlightening occurred. Upon closer scrutiny, the woman realized that she was doing *everything listed* for her second husband. Everything. And she hadn't even realized it.

Why had the duties been a drudgery before, when they were so easy and even enjoyable now? Because now her labor was the fruit of mutual love and respect. Same work. Same Tasks. But now they were a natural response from her heart.

Self-control that emerges from our love for Christ is far from being a slow burn. It is enlivening. A privilege. Something we accept willingly—no matter how long the list!

Faithfulness, or reliability. Gentleness, or consideration of others. Self-control, or self-mastery that makes us into his servants. All are so essential. We need to transport them all over the bridges that he has helped us to build.

Added to the other spiritual fruit that we have described, these are destined to satiate the appetites of our spiritually famished world.

But it all starts with bridge building. We must construct bridges that are strong, that extend to a wide variety of persons, and that transport life-giving fruit of the Spirit.

Jesus cares deeply about bridge building. He demonstrated this countless times throughout history, and in his Word he admonished us to do the same.

Saints of the past accepted his challenge. His disciples. Saint Francis, Martin Luther, John Wesley, some of our own ancestors. These, and so many more, have linked us with the God they faithfully served in spite of dungeon, fire, or sword.

And there are scores of present-day bridge builders. We have heard of their dedicated lives: Billy Graham, who courageously ventured behind the Iron Curtain to preach Christ; Chuck Colson, whose prison ministry has touched the lives of thousands of destitute inmates; Anthony Campolo, whose convicting message has effectively linked the world's impoverished with the vast resources of Christians.

Who could possibly forget Mother Teresa! This tireless, remarkable woman cares for India's poor and dying. Even when on a trip to be honored by our President, this angel of mercy visited Washington, D.C.'s suffering. We would have expected that.

Coming closer to home, most of us realize that we owe much to certain persons who have built bridges to us. They're in our families, friendships, places of employment, churches. Toward them we feel a tremendous sense of gratitude as well as an eternal love-bond.

Furthermore, it inspires our hearts to hear about others who have built Christian bridges.

In the final chapter, allow me to tell three brief stories that will encourage your heart. Perhaps they will motivate you to reach out in love as never before.

You can tell the character of a man by the way he treats those who can do nothing for him.—Dan Reeves

If only all the hands that reach could touch.—Loberg

My wife and I sleep in separate bedrooms, take separate vacations and eat separately at mealtimes. We're doing all we can to keep this marriage together.
—Rodney Dangerfield

12

He Makes the Pieces Fit!

The writer of Proverbs sounds much like a jeweler: "A word aptly spoken is like apples of gold in settings of silver" (25:11).

He is right. Words can conjure up beautiful mindscapes that yield intense pleasure. Also, words can engender great energy, so that perspectives are enlarged and actions motivated.

Nevertheless, as we've all heard, one picture is worth a thousand words.

Vision transcends verbiage. While an absence of words can bring relief (cf. 1 Thess. 4:11), a lack of vision can cause us to perish (cf. Prov. 29:18, KJV).

With this in mind, allow me to show you not one but three pictures. They're not like the photographs we have in our scrapbooks. Rather, they more closely resemble action-filled moving pictures. One scene follows another with eye-blink rapidity. And the providential events combine to yield intense Christian drama.

Not only that. Each story provides a valuable lesson for those of us who commit ourselves to excellent Christian bridge building.

Cranberries, Anyone?

In Ted Engstrom's insightful book, *The Fine Art of Friendship*, he relates a story about his wife Dorothy.

It was the day before Thanksgiving. She rushed to the market to pick up one item, a jar of cranberries.

There was only one jar left on the shelf. As she reached for it, another lady's hand reached out to grasp the same jar. Apparently, she also needed this item to make her Thanksgiving dinner complete.

Each of the ladies insisted that the other take the jar. Finally, the store manager intervened and assured them that there were more jars of cranberries in the stock room.

Was this a happenstance? A chance encounter? A fluke? Not really. Instead, it was the beginning of a friendship that had eternal significance.

Here are the events that quickly transpired. Dorothy offered Bette a favorite recipe, a pink and fluffy cranberry sherbet.

Then, soon after the holidays, the two women began meeting socially. Before long, Bette's husband Ned began stopping by the Engstroms' home to visit.

One day Ned and Bette requested assistance in meeting people in the community, for they had just moved there.

The master bridge-building architect gave his servant Dorothy a plan. She invited Bette to her Christian women's Bible study. This led to an invitation to an afternoon prayer meeting.

Dorothy didn't wish to appear pushy, but the Holy Spirit seemed to be urging her to link Bette to positive, spiritual influences.

At the first afternoon prayer session something marvelous occurred. Bette quietly slipped to her knees, and brushing back tears that ran down her cheeks, asked Jesus to come into her life.

Our Lord only had to be asked once. His presence flooded Bette's heart.

Well, this event occurred over twenty years ago. Today, Bette, Ned and their five children are some of the Engstroms' closest friends. More important, the entire Vessey family has invited Jesus into their lives.

And it all began when two women providentially reached for a lone jar of cranberries![1]

What useful lesson can we learn from this inspiring account? *Bridges can be built just about anywhere and at any time. Therefore, we must be continually perceptive of people's situations, open to them, and prepared to start building.*

Don't Charge *Me* for Your Prayers!

This story did not begin on such a positive, cordial note. I know, because I was there.

The setting was a university classroom. I had been invited to guest lecture to three hundred students.

After being introduced, I did something that is my usual practice. I invited the class to join me in a brief word of prayer. This is perfectly in order at our Christian university.

The prayer couldn't have lasted over thirty seconds. Then my lecture on "Culture" began.

When the class was dismissed, I lingered in front to answer questions of individual students. Several approached me, mainly to clarify certain issues for their notes.

But one student stalked toward me with something else on his mind. It was evident in his eyes and demeanor. He did not wish to ask anything. Instead, he wanted to tell

---

1. Ted W. Engstrom (with Robert C. Larson), *The Fine Art of Friendship* (Nashville, TN: Thomas Nelson Publishers, 1985), pp. 25–26.

me something. Something that made him very upset. His voice was very audible.

This student deeply resented the fact that I had chosen to pray in class. I'll never forget his words. "You used class time to pray, time that I paid money for. I feel robbed!"

Being as nondefensive as I knew how, I invited the young man to my office. He showed up within minutes.

To begin, I asked him to tell me about himself. He seemed to relax a bit as he spoke.

I learned that his family originated in India but currently resided in Hong Kong. They were wealthy. Like him, they did not believe in the views of Christianity, for they were Hindu.

As he spoke, I realized that there were thick layers of walls between us: professor versus student, Indian versus American, wealthy versus not wealthy, Christian versus Hindu. We were continents apart.

I must confess I was too unprepared to say much of anything. I just listened. But that seemed to calm him considerably. When he departed that day, I simply invited him back to talk some more. He seemed shocked, but said that he would come.

And he did. The next time he carried with him a book that he wanted me to read. It was about love from an Eastern religions perspective. Because the book had meant so much to him, I decided to take the time to read it.

In a couple weeks he returned. This time to discuss the book he had given me to read. I assured him that I had found certain parts of the book informative. He seemed very pleased.

Then I asked him if he had ever read the Bible. He assured me that he had not. But more important, he did not assure that he would not. Since I had read his favorite book, he agreed to read mine.

Following this, we met a number of times. I was amazed to see how the young man began to change. The antagonism vanished. He relaxed, and we communicated. At times we would have a hearty laugh together.

My nemesis actually became my friend. Sure, the walls remained, but they became shorter and thinner. We were able to transcend them easily because of Jesus.

Well, our relationship continued, and deepened, for two years. My friend was now a senior. He still was not a Christian, and it seemed that he would not become one. His attention gravitated toward the lucrative family business that he would be heading after his graduation.

As I recall, he had not stopped by my office for several weeks. I assumed that he was in the throes of a hectic year and might not return at all. Nevertheless, I prayed for his spiritual welfare.

At the close of a typical school day, I grabbed my briefcase and began walking toward the car. My thoughts were homeward as I saw the Malibu sun chinning itself on the horizon.

Suddenly, I heard a loud voice calling out from the opposite end of the parking lot. "Dr. Jon, wait a minute!" I looked up, and running toward me with a beaming smile was my Indian friend.

After catching his breath he said the words I wanted to hear "I have accepted Jesus Christ into my heart, and I never knew that it could be so wonderful!"

My heart leaped within me. I could hardly believe what I was hearing. All of the walls collapsed at once. We were now more than friends, we were Christian brothers!

Some Christian students had invited him to a weekend retreat. He had responded to their love and teaching, putting it together with what we had discussed. The Lord had faithfully dealt with his open heart. Praise his name!

Words cannot express the joy I felt that day, greater than if the young man had offered me a million dollars.

A love bridge had been constructed. One that would last forever.

As I drove home, I could only pray that this scene would be repeated over and over again.

Is there a helpful lesson that can be learned from this experience? Yes. *We must relentlessly work at building a bridge, regardless of the other person's reaction and in spite of how long the construction process requires.*

The Undelivered Christmas Present

This story seems as though it could be a best-selling novel. Certainly, all the necessary drama is present.

But unfortunately it isn't fiction. It really occurred. And one of my best friends felt the full, tragic impact.

At the time, Tom was a small boy living in southern California. His father had a severe drinking problem, and the whole family endured the pain.

One evening just before Christmas, Tom's father clutched a present for his son. He was on his way home to deliver it. Anyone seeing him walk could see that he had had too much to drink. He stumbled into the path of an oncoming car, which struck him with terrific force. He lay there motionless. Tom's father was dead.

At this critical time, a kind minister and loving lay-persons reached out. Tom crossed their bridge to the Savior. Jesus became his missing father and changed his life forever.

We attended church youth camps together. He spoke of a divine call to become a minister.

Before long, we found ourselves at the same Christian college. I recall his disciplined study habits and spiritual growth. That pattern continued when we attended seminary.

His mother, still not a Christian, voiced no uncertain objection to the pathway he had chosen. She had greater aspirations for her son, and felt the pain of this denouncement. Nevertheless, he continued his ministerial preparation with an unwavering faith.

After graduating from seminary, he accepted a prestigious ecclesiastical position. This involved traveling throughout the country, speaking, and planning, which he did with expertise and innovation.

His successes, however, led to his demise. Certain superiors felt that he was overzealous, and this seemed to make their jobs more difficult.

In response, my friend was released from his position for being too excellent in his dispatch of duty.

Refusing to give up, he accepted a pastorate. His dreams were big. Unfortunately, so were his failures. In spite of some church growth, the people were not very responsive to him. So the young minister resigned from that church with a heavy heart. He began to seriously wonder about his future.

Eventually, this tenacious servant of God accepted another church. But this time, as never before, he tirelessly labored to build bridges to his members and even more to the needy in the city.

For example, he started a "happy hour" for reformed alcoholics. He and his wife taught a divorce recovery workshop, along with a seminar for single parents. Scores of people attended.

My friend rode night patrol with policemen in order to minister to victims of tragedy.

Many crossed the bridges he had constructed, and began attending the church. The pastor with all the members of the choir would meet them in the parking lot with a heartfelt welcome.

What had been a very small church grew to become the largest in the city.

Why? Because my friend had demonstrated and taught the importance of bridge building. Of getting beyond the church's four walls in order to truly minister.

Concerning the church walls, they had to be greatly expanded. Growth occurred in geometric proportions. Everyone seemed to come to hear "that minister who welcomes you in the parking lot."

Many other churches heard about my friend's success and invited him to be their pastor. He politely withdrew his name. He wasn't interested in climbing any ecclesiastical success ladder. He was content to continue carrying out a fruitful ministry in a needy city.

But, as we might expect, this faithful servant was sensitive to the voice of God. And one day an invitation came that his heavenly Father would not permit him to ignore. A shocked congregation heard him say that he was leaving.

This time he went to a strong church, with the intention of making it stronger. At the time of this writing, my friend has served this church for just over two years. The growth has been remarkable—nearly thirty percent.

What is the precipitant? Again, it is the bridge-building efforts of a minister and his people. They are offering the life-giving fruit of the Spirit to multitudes of needy people. They comb hospital wards. Visit prisoners and shut-ins. And operate nearly two dozen recovery groups that are extended to such persons as substance abusers, divorcees, and the poor.

My friend is now preaching three sermons on Sunday mornings. His church building, again, cannot contain the large crowds.

In spite of this, he continues to greet visitors in the parking lot, cordially welcoming them to the house of God.

And when they enter the doors, church members warmly receive them with a "Where-have-you-been-all-my-life?" look in their eyes.

That's only the beginning. On the following Monday, newcomers receive a plate of warm cookies along with materials that explain the church's programs and ministries.

Soon after, Sunday school teachers, youth leaders, and other laypersons begin to visit. As a body, the entire church extends tender loving care. Could any of us resist this for long?

Well, my friend never received his earthly father's Christmas present that traumatic day. But, on another day—this one triumphant—his heavenly Father will make up for it. For then, he shall receive an eternal reward.

What essential lesson does this minister's story teach us? *Regardless of the pain and resistance we endure, we must refuse to build walls of protection. Instead, our divine imperative is to continue building bridges.*

Three stories. Three lessons. All point to both the possibility and necessity of building bridges to those who need us. And to those we need to serve.

A Parting Word

Jesus built bridges. So *durable* they've lasted for two thousand years. So *diverse* that they connect all human beings with his heavenly Father.

Likewise, he expects us his faithful followers to join the spiritual bridge builder's union. He promises to show and tell us about this important enterprise each step of the way. He shows by his example. He tells by his revealed Word.

Most of us cannot expect to construct bridges as impressive as the ones built by Mother Teresa, Chuck Colson, or Billy Graham. Their "Golden Gates" are beyond our capabilities.

Nevertheless, we can all begin constructing bridges that are commensurate with our God-given capabilities, bridges that

link others with *Jesus*;

connect them with dynamic *ministers*;

bond outsiders with consecrated, Christian *laymen*; and

fuse lonely isolates with *ourselves*.

In so doing, we must constantly remind ourselves that Christian bridge building involves three essential steps: design (construction), destination (connection), delivery (commerce). We have attempted to explain each of these in the three sections of this book.

William Barclay speaks the truth when he emphasizes the importance of relationships for the Christian.

> It is very significant that Christianity began with a group. The Christian faith is something which, from the beginning, had to be discovered and lived out in relationship.[1]

While the ancient Pharisees, whose very name means "separated ones," sought isolation and insulation, Christians have always lived in communion. In oneness. In unity. When we build walls rather than bridges, we are, without a doubt, acting in an un-Christian manner.

Ninety-nine out of one hundred believers will agree with this biblical conclusion. However, becoming dedicated bridge builders is another issue.

Some of us have earnestly, conscientiously attempted to build bridges, but have failed. We've not been adequately trained. When it comes to relationships skills, we're klutzes. Or, we know how to construct only one type of bridge and think that it will suffice for all kinds of people. Or, we build self-designed structures according to our mistake-prone specifications. We refuse to construct them God's way.

Others of us have constructed some pretty decent-looking structures, but have neglected to use them for spiritual commerce. Instead of transporting authentic fruit of the Spirit, we've used our linkages for secular purposes—just to be sociable. To have fun. To avoid being lonely.

Still others of us have been far too selective. We've divided humanity into two categories: designers and ge-

1. *The Daily Study Bible: Gospel of Mark* (Philadelphia: The Westminster Press, 1954), pp. 68–69.

nerics. The first we respond to warmly; the second we avoid like the plague, or we do un-Christlike things such as putting them down ("You are beneath me and my kind"), putting them on ("I'll only let you see what I choose to let you see"), putting them off ("I'll do anything to avoid having an authentic relationship with you").[2]

We must begin today to build bridges. And as we do, grotesque walls in our lives will crumble and collapse.

We have no time to waste, for life is so short. John Wesley's comment is pointed:

> I am a creature of a day, passing through life, as an arrow through the air. I am a spirit come from God, and returning to God; just hovering over the great gulf; until a few months hence, I am no more seen! I will drop into an unchangeable eternity.
>
> I want to know *one* thing, the way to heaven; how to land safely on that happy shore.[3]

What we do we must do quickly. For the time that knows us now will soon know us no more. Bridge building on the double!

But while we're deeply absorbed in our important task, we are well-advised to keep this fact in mind: While we are building bridges *for* God, we are building bridges *to* him.

In short, the linkages we construct to others will become our bridges to heaven's blissful shores. For, by joining God in doing his will, we assure ourselves of the fact that we will someday receive the fullness of his will.

We've talked enough. Excuse me. Will you please hand me that plank?

---

2. Jon Johnston, *Will Evangelicalism Survive Its Own Popularity?* (Grand Rapids, MI: Zondervan Publishing House, 1980), p. 44.

3. John Wesley, Preface to his two volumes of sermons.

Stanford Shyness Survey

T his is a version of the survey that we gave to over 5,000 people around the world. Fill it out quickly, then go back over it more carefully to see how exactly shyness affects your life. This is not a scored test, rather it is intended to stimulate self-appraisal and group discussion.

_____ 1. Do you consider yourself to be a shy person?
    1 = yes
    2 = no

_____ 2. If yes, have you always been shy (were shy previously and still are)?
    1 = yes
    2 = no

_____ 3. If no to question 1, was there *ever* a prior time in your life when you were shy?
    1 = yes
    2 = no

    If no, then you are finished with this survey. Thank you.
    If yes to any of the above, please continue.

_____ 4. How shy are you when you feel shy?
    1 = extremely shy
    2 = very shy

3 = quite shy
4 = moderately shy
5 = somewhat shy
6 = only slightly shy

_____ 5. How often do you experience (have you experienced) these feelings of shyness?
1 = every day
2 = almost every day
3 = often, nearly every other day
4 = one or two times a week
5 = occasionally, less than once a week
6 = rarely, once a month or less

_____ 6. Compared with your peers (of similar age, sex, and background), how shy are you?
1 = much more shy
2 = more shy
3 = about as shy
4 = less shy
5 = much less shy

_____ 7. How desirable is it for you to be shy?
1 = very undesirable
2 = undesirable
3 = neither desirable nor undesirable
4 = desirable
5 = very desirable

_____ 8. Is (or was) your shyness ever a personal problem for you?
1 = yes, often
2 = yes, sometimes
3 = yes, occasionally
4 = rarely
5 = never

_____ 9. When you are feeling shy, can you conceal it and have others believe you are not feeling shy?
1 = yes, always

2 = sometimes I can, sometimes not
3 = no, I usually can't hide it

_____ 10. Do you consider yourself more of an introvert or an extrovert?
1 = strongly introverted
2 = moderately introverted
3 = slightly introverted
4 = neither
5 = slightly extroverted
6 = moderately extroverted
7 = strongly extroverted

(11–19) Which of the following do you believe may be among the causes of your shyness? Check all that are applicable to you.

_____ 11. Concern for negative evaluation

_____ 12. Fear of being rejected

_____ 13. Lack of self-confidence

_____ 14. Lack of specific skills (specify): _____
_____

_____ 15. Fear of being intimate with others

_____ 16. Preference for being alone

_____ 17. Value placed on nonsocial interests, hobbies, etc.

_____ 18. Personal inadequacy, handicap (specify): _____
_____
_____

_____ 19. Others (specify): _____
_____
_____

(20–27) Perceptions of your shyness
Do the following people consider you to be shy? How shy do you think they judge you to be? Answer using this scale.

1 = extremely shy
2 = very shy
3 = quite shy
4 = moderately shy
5 = somewhat shy
6 = only slightly shy
7 = not shy
8 = don't know
9 = not applicable

_____ 20. your mother

_____ 21. your father

_____ 22. your siblings (brothers and/or sisters)

_____ 23. close friends

_____ 24. your steady boy/girlfriend or spouse

_____ 25. your high-school classmates

_____ 26. your current roommate

_____ 27. teachers, employers, or fellow workers who know you well

_____ 28. In deciding whether or not to call yourself a shy person, was your decision based on the fact that:
1 = you are (were) shy all of the time in all situations
2 = you are (were) shy at least 50 percent of the time, in more situations than not
3 = you are (were) shy only occasionally, but those occasions are (were) of enough importance to justify calling yourself a shy person

_____ 29. Have people ever misinterpreted your shyness as being a different trait such as indifference, aloofness, poise?
1 = yes

Specify: _____

_____

2 = no

_____ 30. Do you ever feel shy when you are alone?
1 = yes
2 = no

_____ 31. Do you ever feel embarrassed when you are alone?
1 = yes
2 = no

_____ 32. If yes, describe when, how, or why:

_____

_____

(33–36) What makes you shy?

_____ 33. If you now experience or have ever experienced feelings of shyness, indicate which of the following situations, activities, and types of people make you feel shy. Place a check mark next to all of the appropriate choices.

Situations and activities that make me feel shy:

_____ social situations in general
_____ large groups
_____ small, task-oriented groups (e.g., seminars at school, work groups on the job)
_____ small social groups (e.g., parties, dances)
_____ one-to-one interactions with a person of the same sex
_____ one-to-one interactions with a person of the opposite sex
_____ situations where I am vulnerable (e.g., when asking for help)

_____ situations where I am of lower status than others (e.g., when speaking to superiors, authorities)

_____ situations requiring assertiveness (e.g., when complaining about faulty service in a restaurant or the poor quality of a product)

_____ situations where I am the focus of attention before a large group (e.g., when giving a speech)

_____ situations where I am the focus of attention before a small group (e.g., when being introduced, when being asked directly for my opinion)

_____ situations where I am being evaluated or compared with others (e.g., when being interviewed, when being criticized)

_____ new interpersonal situations in general

_____ where sexual intimacy is possible

34. Now go back and indicate next to each item you checked whether your shyness has been elicited in the past month by this situation or activity:
    0 = not in the past month, but prior
    1 = yes, very strongly
    2 = yes, strongly so
    3 = moderately so
    4 = only mildly
    5 = not at all

35. Types of people who make me feel shy:
    _____ my parents
    _____ my siblings (brothers and/or sisters)
    _____ other relatives
    _____ friends
    _____ strangers

_____ foreigners
_____ authorities (by virtue of their role—
police, teachers, superior at work)
_____ authorities (by virtue of their knowledge—intellectual superiors, experts)
_____ elderly people (much older than I)
_____ children (much younger than I)
_____ persons of the opposite sex, in a
group
_____ persons of the same sex, in a group
_____ a person of the opposite sex, one-to-
one
_____ a person of the same sex, one-to-one

36. Now go back and indicate next to each one
you checked under 35 whether your shyness
has been elicited in the past month by this
person (or type of person):
0 = not in the past month but prior
1 = yes, very strongly
2 = yes, strongly so
3 = moderately so
4 = only mildly

(37–40)   Shyness reactions

_____ 37. How do you know you are shy; that is, what
cues do you use?
1 = my internal feelings, thoughts, symp-
toms only (private)
2 = my overt behavior in a given situation
only (public)
3 = I use a mix of internal responses and
overt behavior

Physical reactions

38. If you do experience or have ever experienced
feelings of shyness, which of the following
physical reactions are associated with such

feelings? Put 0 next to those that are not relevant, then order the rest from 1 (most typical, usual, severe) to 2 (next most), and so on, or: –be more specific.

_____ blushing
_____ increased pulse
_____ butterflies in stomach
_____ tingling sensations
_____ heart pounding
_____ dry mouth
_____ tremors
_____ perspiration
_____ fatigue
_____ others (specify): _____
  _____
  _____
  _____

Thoughts, feelings

39. What are the specific thoughts and sensations associated with your shyness? Put 0 next to those that are not relevant, then order the rest from 1 (most typical, usual, severe) to 2 (next most), and so on. More than one item can be given the same rank.

_____ positive thoughts (e.g., feeling content with myself)

_____ no specific thoughts (e.g., daydreaming, thinking about nothing in particular)

_____ self-conciousness (e.g., an extreme awareness of myself, of my every action)

_____ thoughts that focus on the unpleasantness of the situation (e.g., thinking that the situation is terrible, thinking that I'd like to be out of the situation)

_____ thoughts that provide distractions (e.g., thinking of other things that I could be doing, thinking that the experience will be over in a short while)

_____ negative thoughts about myself (e.g., feeling inadequate, insecure, inferior, stupid)

_____ thoughts about the evaluation of me that others are making (e.g., wondering what the people around me are thinking of me)

_____ thoughts about the way in which I am handling myself (e.g., wondering what kind of impression I am creating and how I might control it)

_____ thoughts about shyness in general (e.g., thinking about the extent of my shyness and its consequences, wishing that I weren't shy)

_____ others (specify): _____

_____

Actions

40. If you do experience or have ever experienced feelings of shyness, what are the obvious behaviors which might indicate to others that you are feeling shy? Put 0 next to those that are not relevant, then rank order the rest from 1 (most typical, usual, severe) to 2 (next most), and so on. More than one item can be given the same rank.

_____ low speaking voice

_____ avoidance of other people

_____ inability to make eye contact

_____ silence (a reluctance to talk)

_____ stuttering

_____ rambling, incoherent talk

_____ posture

_____ avoidance of taking action

_____ escape from the situation

_____ others (specify): _____

_____

_____

(41–42)   Shyness consequences

    41. What are the negative consequences of being shy? Check all those that apply to you.

_____ none, no negative consequences

_____ creates social problems; makes it difficult to meet new people, make new friends, enjoy potentially good experiences

_____ has negative emotional consequences; creates feeling of loneliness, isolation, depression

_____ prevents positive evaluations by others (e.g., my personal assets never become apparent because of my shyness)

_____ makes it difficult to be appropriately assertive, to express opinions, to take advantage of opportunities

_____ allows incorrect negative evaluations by others (e.g., I may unjustly be seen as unfriendly or snobbish or weak)

_____ creates cognitive and expressive difficulties; inhibits the capacity to think clearly while with others and to communicate effectively with them

_____ encourages excessive self-consciousness, preoccupation with myself

    42. What are the positive consequences of being shy? Check all those that apply to you.

_____ none, no positive consequences

_____ creates a modest, appealing impression; makes one appear discrete, introspective

_____ helps avoid interpersonal conflicts

_____ provides a convenient form of anonymity and protection

_____ provides an opportunity to stand back, observe others, act carefully and intelligently

_____ avoids negative evaluations by others (e.g., a shy person is not considered obnoxious, overaggressive, or pretentious)

_____ provides a way to be selective about the people with whom one interacts

_____ enhances personal privacy and the pleasure that solitude offers

_____ creates positive interpersonal consequences by not putting others off, intimidating them, or hurting them

_____ 43. Do you think your shyness can be overcome?
1 = yes
2 = no
3 = uncertain

_____ 44. Are you willing to seriously work at overcoming it?
1 = yes, definitely
2 = yes, perhaps
3 = not sure yet
4 = no

Appendix **2**

Stress Rating the Effects of Forty-Three Personal Crises

Background

In the 1920's, Dr. Walter Cannon began recording connections between stressful periods in a person's life and the appearance of physical ailments. A decade later, Dr. Adolf Meyer compiled a life chart which specifically correlated health problems with a person's particular life circumstances at the time. This process was refined during the 1950s and 1960s, and resulted in the creation of the Social Readjustment Rating Scale (SRRS), which ranks 43 life crises on a scale of Life Change Units (LCUs). The ratings were arrived at by researchers who used indepth interviewing techniques on an international sample of 5,000 people from Europe, the U.S., Central America, Oceania, and Japan. Because of the consistency with which marriage was rated as one of the most significant life changes, it was given a value of 50 on the scale, and 42 other life crises were judged in relation to it. Some cultural differences surfaced (for example, the Japanese ranked minor law violations near the middle of the list and jail terms second from the top), but on the whole there was a remarkable uniformity of results, cutting across all national and socioeconomic levels. SRRS supporters contend that there is a direct correlation between annual LCUs and stress-related diseases. One of their studies found that with a mild stress level (150–199 LCUs in a single year), health problems increased 37% above the average; with a moderate level (200–299 LCUs), the increase was 51%; and with major crisis level (300 LCUs and above), 79% more health problems occurred. The researchers noted that what counted was the cumulative total, not whether the life changes in themselves were positive or negative.

Rank	Life Event	LCU Value
1.	Death of a spouse	100
2.	Divorce	73
3.	Marital separation	65
4.	Jail term	63
4.	Death of a close family member	63
6.	Personal injury or illness	53
7.	Marriage	50
8.	Fired from job	47
9.	Marital reconciliation	45
9.	Retirement	45
11.	Change in health of family member	44
12.	Pregnancy	40
13.	Sex difficulties	39
13.	Gain of a new family member	39
13.	Business readjustment	39
16.	Change in financial state	38
17.	Death of a close friend	37
18.	Change to a different line of work	36
19.	Change in number of arguments with spouse	35
20.	Mortgage over $10,000	31
21.	Foreclosure on mortgage or loan	30
22.	Change in responsibilities at work	29
22.	Son or daughter leaving home	29
22.	Trouble with in-laws	29
25.	Outstanding personal achievement	28

28		
26.	Wife begins or stops working	26
26.	Beginning or end of school	26
28.	Change in living conditions	25
29.	Revision of personal habits	24
30.	Trouble with boss	23
31.	Change in work hours or conditions	20
31.	Change in residence	20
31.	Change in schools	20
34.	Change in recreation	19
34.	Change in church activities	19
36.	Change in social activities	18
37.	Mortgage or loan less than $10,000	17
38.	Change in sleeping habits	16
39.	Change in number of family get-togethers	15
39.	Change in eating habits	15
41.	Vacation	13
42.	Christmas	12
43.	Minor violations of the law	11

Appendix **3**

Highest and Lowest Pressure Jobs in the U.S.A.

In the two-year study conducted by NIOSH (National Institute for Occupational Safety and Health) in cooperation with the Tennessee Department of Mental Health and Mental Retardation, over 22,000 health records of workers in 130 occupations were analyzed with respect to stress-related diseases. The frequency with which these diseases occurred in the various occupations resulted in the following determination of the highest- and lowest-stress jobs.

Highest-pressure Jobs

1. Manual laborer
2. Secretary
3. Inspector
4. Waitress-waiter
5. Clinical lab technician
6. Farm owner
7. Miner
8. Office manager
9. House painter

10. Manager-administrator
11. Foreman
12. Machine operator

Lowest-pressure Jobs

1. Clothing sewer
2. Checker, examiner of products
3. Stockroom worker
4. Craftsman
5. Maid
6. Heavy-equipment operator
7. Farm laborer
8. Freight handler
9. Child care worker
10. Packer, wrapper in shipping
11. College or university professor
12. Personnel, labor relations
13. Auctioneer-huckster

Source: *Occupational Stress*, U.S. Department of Health, Education, and Welfare, National Institute for Occupational Safety and Health, 1978.

Subject Index

Scripture Index

248